T0129192

The CLI Book

Writing Successful Command Line Interfaces with Node.js

Robert Kowalski

Apress®

The CLI Book

Robert Kowalski
Hamburg, Germany

ISBN-13 (pbk): 978-1-4842-3176-0   ISBN-13 (electronic): 978-1-4842-3177-7
https://doi.org/10.1007/978-1-4842-3177-7

Library of Congress Control Number: 2017962012

Cover image designed by Freepik

Managing Director: Welmoed Spahr
Editorial Director: Todd Green
Acquisitions Editor: Louise Corrigan
Development Editor: James Markham
Technical Reviewer: Massimo Nardone
Coordinating Editor: Nancy Chen
Copy Editor: Sharon Wilkey
Compositor: SPi Global
Indexer: SPi Global
Artist: SPi Global

Distributed to the book trade worldwide by Springer Science + Business Media New York, 233 Spring Street, 6th Floor, New York, NY 10013. Phone 1-800-SPRINGER, fax (201) 348-4505, e-mail orders-ny@springer-sbm.com, or visit www.springeronline.com. Apress Media, LLC is a California LLC and the sole member (owner) is Springer Science + Business Media Finance Inc (SSBM Finance Inc). SSBM Finance Inc is a **Delaware** corporation.

For information on translations, please e-mail rights@apress.com, or visit www.apress.com/rights-permissions.

Apress titles may be purchased in bulk for academic, corporate, or promotional use. eBook versions and licenses are also available for most titles. For more information, reference our Print and eBook Bulk Sales web page at www.apress.com/bulk-sales.

Any source code or other supplementary material referenced by the author in this book is available to readers on GitHub via the book's product page, located at www.apress.com/9781484231760. For more detailed information, please visit www.apress.com/source-code.

Printed on acid-free paper

Table of Contents

About the Author vii

About the Technical Reviewer ix

Preface xi

Acknowledgments xiii

Chapter 1: What Makes a Good CLI? 1

  CLI Basics 1

  You Never Get Stuck 2

    Still Lost? Man Pages Will Help 4

    Error Handling 7

  It Supports Power Users 8

    Shortcuts 8

    Scripting 9

    Configuration 11

  You Can Use It for So Many Things! 12

  Summary 13

Chapter 2: Writing a Database Administration Tool with Node.js 15

  Why Use Node.js? 16

  Setting Up the Database Server 16

    Setting Up 16

    Using the PouchDB Database Server 17

    Troubleshooting 18

Performing a Simple Status Check 21

  Starting from Scratch 21

  A Helping Ecosystem 23

  The Internals of the isonline Command 26

  The CLI Part 29

Booting the Tool 31

  Making Sure Lounger Is Loaded 31

  A Nice Way to Interact from the Command Line 36

Summary..38

Chapter 3: Making Our CLI More Accessible 39

Error Handling...39

  Handling Usage Errors...41

  Providing Further Guidance 44

JSON Support and Shorthand 47

Documentation..50

  Rendering the Documentation...52

  Providing HTML Output..58

More Help...66

  General Help with a List of Commands 66

  Help for Each Command 68

Configuration...71

  Creating the Configuration File...71

  The Heart of Our Configuration System...72

  A Helper to Edit the Configuration 76

Our First Release and Tips 80

Summary..82

Chapter 4: Migrating Large Amounts of Data by Using Streams 83

The cat Command 84

The First Stream 85

The Transform and Writable Stream 87

    Creating a Wrapping Transform Stream 88

    Piping the Results into a Writable Stream 91

The Streaming Import Command 95

    Designing the Command 98

    Creating the Target Database 98

Summary 104

APPENDIX A: Tips and Tricks 105

Testing 105

Semantic Versioning with SemVer 105

Greenkeeper 106

Index 107

About the Author

Robert Kowalski started using Node.js when version 0.4 was still new. He has spent time working on the npm core team, which is where he learned a lot about good command-line interfaces. As a developer, he has also had to use other command-line tools, and it was this that made him realize how much a book like this was needed. In the past, he has worked for big companies such as IBM and startups including Jimdo and Bitfinex, all in different roles, as well as committing to Node.js and Apache CouchDB. He speaks at conferences and has enjoyed writing since he was a child. You can find Robert on Twitter. @robinson_k.

About the Technical Reviewer

Massimo Nardone has more than 22 years of experience in security, web/mobile development, the cloud, and IT architecture. His true IT passions are security and Android.

He has been programming and teaching how to program with Android, Perl, PHP, Java, VB, Python, C/C++, and MySQL for more than 20 years.

He holds a master of science degree in computing science from the University of Salerno, Italy. He has worked as a project manager, software engineer, research engineer, chief security architect, information security manager, PCI/SCADA auditor, and senior lead IT security/cloud/SCADA architect for many years.

Technical skills include security, Android, cloud, Java, MySQL, Drupal, Cobol, Perl, web and mobile development, MongoDB, D3, Joomla, Couchbase, C/C++, WebGL, Python, Pro Rails, Django CMS, Jekyll, and Scratch.

He currently works as chief information security officer (CISO) for Cargotec Oyj. He has also worked as a visiting lecturer and supervisor for exercises at the Networking Laboratory of the Helsinki University of Technology (Aalto University). He holds four international patents (PKI, SIP, SAML, and Proxy areas).

Massimo has reviewed more than 40 IT books for various publishing companies. He is the coauthor of *Pro Android Games* (Apress, 2015).

Preface

Command-line clients are everywhere. Almost everyone, at least in tech, is using them.

Many successful command-line clients are available: the Linux project has Git, and the Node.js project has npm. We use some of them multiple times a day. Apache CouchDB recently got nmo (pronounced *nemo*), a tool to manage the database cluster. We can learn a lot from successful command-line interfaces in order to write better command-line clients.

When I started to become interested in command-line clients, I realized that the Web hosts a lot of discussions and information about writing APIs. The Web is full of tutorials that can teach you how to build APIs, especially REST APIs, but almost nothing can be found about writing good command-line interfaces (CLIs). This book explains what makes a good CLI. In the second part of the book, you will build a small command-line client to learn how to use Node.js to create great command-line clients that people love.

The goal of the book is to show the principles for building a successful command-line client. The provided code should give you a good understanding of what is important to build successful command-line clients and how to implement them.

Every section has its own code examples. Before you run the code, you have to run `npm install` in the folder provided for that section.

You can download the code samples from `https://github.com/theclibook/theclibook/archive/1.0.zip`.

I hope you enjoy the book.

Acknowledgments

I want to thank Michelle Phung and Klaus Trainer for their input on the very first version of this book.

I'm also deeply indebted to Isaac Schlueter, who merged my first patch to npm. Without your support, I wouldn't have dived into the art of great command-line interfaces. This is also the right place to thank Domenic Denicola for his impact on my work over the years.

Big thanks to Louise Corrigan, Nancy Chen, Massimo Nardone, and James Markham from Apress for their kind feedback and support.

I also have to thank my family: my parents, for the invaluable support they provided since I was born. My sister, for being a wonderful sister. I hope this book makes you proud!

CHAPTER 1

What Makes a Good CLI?

In this chapter, you'll take a look at successful command-line clients and what they do well. This will help you understand the problems users face, and thus help you build better command-line clients with Node.js later in the book.

CLI Basics

Let's first take a look at how users typically use a command-line interface (CLI). Most of the time, users sit in front of a keyboard and interact with a terminal. You should use simple and recognizable commands for the CLI. But sadly, just using easily recognizable commands won't get you far enough.

The problem will be easier to understand if you take a look at a bad CLI:

```
$ my-example-cli -A -a 16 r foo.html
error: undefined is not a function
```

In this example, you have to enter cryptic commands that are then answered by a cryptic error message. You might ask, "What does -A -a 16 r mean?" and "Why I am getting an error back; am I using it wrong?" and "What does the error mean, and how can I get my task done?"

© Robert Kowalski 2017
R. Kowalski, *The CLI Book*, https://doi.org/10.1007/978-1-4842-3177-7_1

So what makes a good CLI? In short, a successful CLI is one that makes users successful and happy.

Let's try creating a CLI by using the following three principles:

- You never get stuck in the CLI.

- It is simple and supports power users.

- You can use it for so many things.

You Never Get Stuck

Nobody likes to be in a traffic jam, stuck, just moving a few feet each minute. You want to reach your target destination in the fastest and most comfortable way. The same applies to your users: they become extremely unhappy when tools are standing in their way. They just want to get their tasks done.

Never getting stuck means that you should always offer your users a way to solve their tasks. A command should never be a dead end. Additionally, you should avoid every source of friction in your command-line tool.

To better illustrate this, let's take a look at Git and npm—two very successful command-line tools.

The following example uses Git:

```
$ git poll
git: 'poll' is not a git command. See 'git --help'.

Did you mean this?

pull
```

In this example, I entered the wrong command, poll, instead of pull. Fortunately, Git offers a way to continue my work and finish the task.

Git is basically saying, "Hey, Robert, it looks like you entered the wrong command, but if you type in git --help, you can see a list of all the existing commands. And, hey, it looks like you typed git poll; did you mean git pull?"

npm, another successful CLI client, offers the same concept:

```
$ npm ragrragr
Usage: npm <command>

where <command> is one of:
    access, add-user, adduser, apihelp, author, bin, bugs, c,
    cache, completion, config, ddp, dedupe, deprecate, dist-tag,
    dist-tags, docs, edit, explore, faq, find, find-dupes, get,
    help, help-search, home, i, info, init, install, issues, la,
    link, list, ll, ln, login, logout, ls, outdated, owner,
    pack, prefix, prune, publish, r, rb, rebuild, remove, repo,
    restart, rm, root, run-script, s, se, search, set, show,
    shrinkwrap, star, stars, start, stop, t, tag, test, tst, un,
    uninstall, unlink, unpublish, unstar, up, update, upgrade,
    v, verison, version, view, whoami

npm <cmd> -h     quick help on <cmd>
npm -l           display full usage info
npm faq          commonly asked questions
npm help <term>  search for help on <term>
npm help npm     involved overview

Specify configs in the ini-formatted file:
    /Users/robert/.npmrc
or on the command line via: npm <command> —key value
Config info can be viewed via: npm help config

npm@5.5.1 /Users/robert/.nvm/versions/node/v9.1.0/lib/node_
modules/npm
```

In this example, I tried to put garbage into npm, so npm offers some friendly help: "Hey, Robert, I don't know that command, but here are all the commands that are possible. You can use them like this and get help about them by typing in npm help <command>."

Like Git, npm immediately offers help to enable me to finish my task, even if I have no idea how to use npm at all.

Still Lost? Man Pages Will Help

What if I still need help? Maybe I want to get help before trying out any commands. Turns out, there's a reliable way to find documentation on Unix or Linux: manual pages, or *man pages*, shown in Figure 1-1.

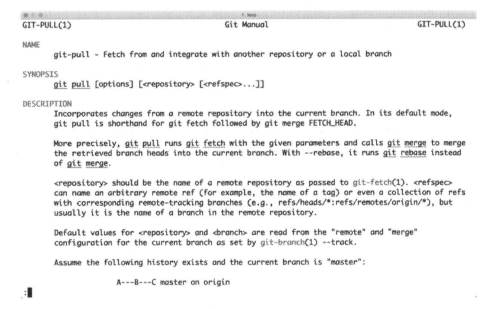

Figure 1-1. The man page for git pull

Man pages are quite nice, as you don't need the Internet to open them. You can also stay in the same terminal window to read them and don't have to switch to another window (such as a. a browser).

But some users don't know about man pages or don't like to use them. Others will be working on Windows, which can't handle man pages natively, so Git and npm offer their documentation as web pages, as shown in Figure 1-2.

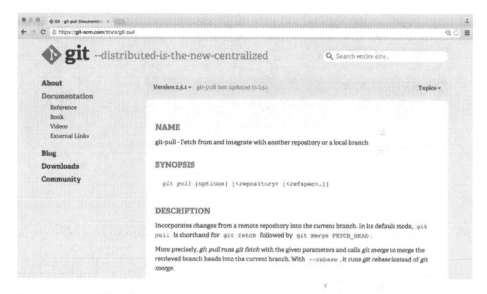

Figure 1-2. *The documentation web site of the Git project*

Both Git and npm use a trick: they write their documentation once (for example, in Markdown or AsciiDoc) and use that initial source as a base. Later, they convert those base documents to different formats (for example, to HTML).

If you look at the online man pages of Git and npm, you will notice that their web sites frame the content with a header and a sidebar. Figure 1-3 and Figure 1-4 illustrate this with the different versions for the command `npm publish`.

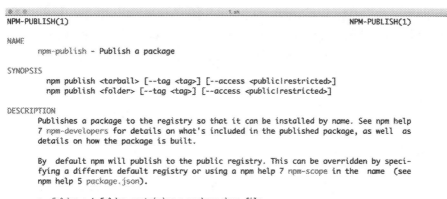

```
NPM-PUBLISH(1)                                                    NPM-PUBLISH(1)

NAME
       npm-publish - Publish a package

SYNOPSIS
          npm publish <tarball> [--tag <tag>] [--access <public|restricted>]
          npm publish <folder> [--tag <tag>] [--access <public|restricted>]

DESCRIPTION
          Publishes a package to the registry so that it can be installed by name. See npm help
          7 npm-developers for details on what's included in the published package, as well  as
          details on how the package is built.

          By  default npm will publish to the public registry. This can be overridden by speci-
          fying a different default registry or using a npm help 7 npm-scope in the  name  (see
          npm help 5 package.json).

          o <folder>: A folder containing a package.json file

          o <tarball>:  A  url or file path to a gzipped tar archive containing a single folder
          with a package.json file inside.

          o [--tag <tag>] Registers the published package with the given  tag,  such  that  npm
          install  <name>@<tag>  will  install this version.  By default, npm publish updates
          and npm install installs the latest tag.
```

Figure 1-3. *The man page for npm publish*

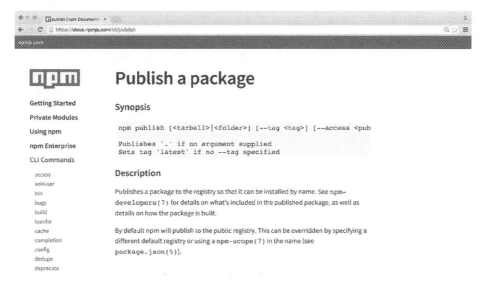

Figure 1-4. *The documentation web site for npm publish*

Error Handling

Sometimes things go still horribly wrong. Let's look at my example of a bad
CLI again:

```
$ my-example-cli -A -a 16 r foo.py
events.js:85
      throw er; // Unhandled 'error' event
          ^
Error: ENOENT, open 'cli.js'
   at Error (native)
```

In this case, you are getting back a stacktrace without much context.
For most people, these stacktraces look cryptic, especially for people who
don't write Node.js on a daily basis.

And it is even worse: you really can't tell whether you just hit a bug in
the CLI or you are using the it in the wrong way. Imagine your users in this
situation. Looking at that small terminal, with no idea what to do, they get
extremely frustrated.

One thing nmo supports is *usage errors*. Here is what they look like:

```
$ nmo cluster dsf
ERR! Usage:

nmo cluster get [<clustername>], [<nodename>]
nmo cluster add <nodename>, <url>, <clustername>
nmo cluster join <clustername>
```

If a user tries to use a command in the wrong way, nmo will indicate
immediately how to use the command to get the job done. No need to
open the documentation.

nmo also shows stacktraces to a user if nmo crashes:

```
$ nmo cluster join anemone
ERR! df is not defined
ERR! ReferenceError: df is not defined
ERR!      at /Users/robert/apache/nmo/lib/cluster.js:84:5
ERR!      at cli (/Users/robert/apache/nmo/lib/cluster.js:68:27)
ERR!      at /Users/robert/apache/nmo/bin/nmo-cli.js:32:6
ERR!
ERR! nmo: 1.0.1 node: v9.1.0
ERR! please open an issue including this log on https://github.
com/robertkowalski/nmo/issues
```

nmo adds the current nmo and Node.js version to the stacktrace, as npm does. We also ask the user to copy the stacktrace and to open an issue containing the stacktrace.

The reports make it easy for a team to identify the bug, solve it, and release a new version of nmo by seeing the stacktrace.

And, again, the user is not stuck. The user gets help to solve the task, and in the worst case, you help the user through your issue tracker.

It Supports Power Users

Power users are important for your CLI. They are the users who will talk about your CLI and increase its overall adoption by spreading the word. The following subsections cover ways to improve interactions with power users.

Shortcuts

Most power users use your CLI multiple times every day. An easy way to support them is to provide shortcuts.

npm has lots of shortcuts. For instance, npm i is the short form for npm install. Git lets you define your own shortcuts in the .gitconfig file. I use git co as a shortcut for git checkout, for example.

Scripting

At some point, your command-line client will become very successful; people will love it and start using it in creative ways. The CLI will suddenly run on Jenkins, as part of deployment in a Chef or Puppet run, or your users will use your CLI in ways you never could have imagined!

Sooner or later, automated processes will also use your CLI. To make your CLI even more successful, it's a good idea to support scripting.

Exit Codes

Operating systems use exit codes to signal whether a command was successful. You will get back a 0 if your recent command was successful. Getting back a 1 indicates a general error.

Exit codes are useful for users who want to wrap your command-line client in a bash script.

Here is an example:

```
$ git poll
git: 'poll' is not a git command. See 'git --help'.
Did you mean this?
  pull
$ echo $?
1
```

Git notifies you that something went wrong; you are getting back a 1 as the exit code. With proper exit codes, every writer of a bash script can handle unsuccessful commands.

JSON Output

In nmo, every command that gives back information supports JSON-formatted output:

```
$ nmo cluster get --json
{ anemone:
   { node1: 'http://node1.local',
     node2: 'http://node2.local',
     node3: 'http://node3.local' } }
```

JSON support enables users to process data easily in the programming language of their choice, as most languages support JSON. Users can spawn a child process in language x and listen to stdout for the output. They can also directly pipe the output into a consumer on the shell:

```
$ nmo cluster get --json | consumer.py
```

JSON output gives users a lot of flexibility.

The API in the Command-Line Client

Another concept can make scripting easier. I call it the *API in the command-line client*:

```
const nmo = require('nmo');

nmo.load({}).then(() => {
  nmo.commands.cluster
    .get('testcluster', 'node1@127.0.01')
    .then((res) => {
      console.log(res);
    });
});
```

In nmo, every command is exposed on `nmo.commands`. If a user wants to use nmo as part of their node scripts, they are able to require it. The JavaScript API is documented like the CLI.

The JavaScript API enables users to embed nmo in their Node.js scripts for complex processes. They could even fork nmo and embed it into their own command-line client.

Configuration

Power users love configuration. Because they use command-line clients a lot, maybe multiple times a day, it is no surprise that they want some features enabled by default. But in rare cases, they don't want the default setting.

npm supports option arguments on the command line:

```
$ npm i hapi --registry=https://reg.example.org
/Users/robert
└── hapi@9.0.4
```

This command downloads the package `hapi` from a private registry at `https://reg.example.org`.

But I can also set this private registry as the new default registry:

```
$ npm config set registry https://reg.example.org
```

npm writes the new registry into the config:

```
$ cat ~/.npmrc
loglevel=http
registry=https://reg.example.org
```

The next time I try to install a package, npm will use my new default registry, `https://reg.example.org`:

```
$ npm i hapi
```

If I don't want to use this new default registry, I can pass an argument to the CLI, and it will use the alternate registry just for this call:

```
$ npm i hapi --registry=https://registry.npmjs.org
/Users/robert
└── hapi@9.0.4
```

That means we have choices between default configurations and command-line arguments in npm, and this combination is extremely powerful.

You Can Use It for So Many Things!

Let's take a look at the last principle: you can use a CLI for so many things. Whenever I have to do a task multiple times, and it fits into the domain of my command-line client, I'll just add it as a new command. This habit turns into a win-win situation: you have to do fewer boring tasks, and your users are happy because they get a new feature and also have to do fewer monkey tasks. This makes your command-line client even more successful.

Let's take npm as an example. When npm was in its early days, it didn't have a command for listing outdated packages. You had to run a full update for all packages and then check which packages were updated and which were not. The addition of the command scratched an itch for its author, but also for all users of npm. Sadly, it can be quite hard to spot common pain points, especially if you work with multiple teams or a lot of people. Additionally, most of us are suffering organizational blindness after working on the same topic for a long time. But if you identify a task that you can automate for you and your users, you will be hugely rewarded!

Summary

Most issues with command-line interfaces are not related to technical problems. Your users should always have an idea about the next steps, especially if things go wrong. Observing someone who uses your CLI for the first time can help you get new ideas for improvements. It's important to have a solid base to be able to attract first users.

As soon as a solid user experience exists, additions such as shortcuts make your CLI more interesting. Power users, especially, will love them.

CHAPTER 2

Writing a Database Administration Tool with Node.js

In this chapter, we will write a database administration tool named lounger and follow the principles that make a good CLI. The code for every section is available at `https://github.com/theclibook/theclibook/tree/1.0/sourcecode`, which you can access via a link at the end of each section. The main repository is at `https://github.com/theclibook/theclibook`. If you want to play with the code, don't forget to run `npm install` in the folder for the section you want to test. The code also has a test suite that you can run with `npm test`.

We'll start with the setup of the development environment. We'll install and start a small PouchDB instance. Then we'll create our first command. To make the command-line tool extensible, we'll also add a bootstrapping part. With a proper bootstrap, we'll load every command and configuration that we add over time. We'll finish the chapter with a first runnable version of the tool that we'll be able to execute on the command line.

© Robert Kowalski 2017
R. Kowalski, *The CLI Book*, https://doi.org/10.1007/978-1-4842-3177-7_2

Why Use Node.js?

I sometimes get asked why I write command-line clients using Node.js. For me, the main reasons are as follows:

- A huge ecosystem with modules in every flavor

- Fast development speed

- Writing JavaScript is fun!

For me, these reasons make Node.js the perfect platform for writing command-line clients.

Setting Up the Database Server

Our first step is to get the database server squared away. This involves a setup process, PouchDB installation, and a bit of troubleshooting.

Setting Up

We will write our command-line client in ES6/7, which brings a lot of improvements to JavaScript. In order to use it, we have to install Node 8.*x* from `https://nodejs.org`. If you want to support older Node.js versions, I recommend the Babel transpiler to transpile the code to ES5-compatible code. You can get Babel at `https://babeljs.io/`.

The tool that we'll write will be a small database administration tool for CouchDB/PouchDB. There are multiple ways to get a development database server up and running.

One way is to install Erlang and CouchDB for your operating system. You can download official packages from `http://couchdb.apache.org`, and many Linux distributions have CouchDB in their package repositories too.

I think the easiest way is to either use the PouchDB server that is available in the source code for this book or to get a CouchDB instance at https://cloudant.com, which is free until you hit a limit.

Using the PouchDB Database Server

The PouchDB database server is located in sourcecode/database. In order to use it, we have to install the needed dependencies:

```
$ cd sourcecode/database
$ npm install
```

To boot the database, we just run the following:

```
$ npm run start
```

We can now interact with the database server via HTTP, as CouchDB and PouchDB are databases with an HTTP API. If you don't know how to get curl, take a look at the following "Troubleshooting" section.

```
$ curl -XGET http://127.0.0.1:5984/
```

```
{"express-pouchdb":"Welcome!","version":"1.0.1","vendor":
{"name":"PouchDB authors","version":"1.0.1"},"uuid":"4fad2c01-
ba32-4249-8278-8786e877c397"}
```

Let's create a database called people:

```
$ curl -XPUT http://127.0.0.1:5984/people
```

```
{"ok":true}
```

We can now insert documents into our people database:

```
$ curl -XPOST http://127.0.0.1:5984/people -d '{"name":
"Rocko Artischocko", \
```

```
 "likes": ["Burritos", "Node.js", "Music"] }' -H 'Content-Type:
application/json'
```

```
{"ok":true,"id":"21b5ad83-0ad6-47c7-86f8d9636113160a","rev":
"1-411894affa038a6fd7a164e1bfd84146"}
```

Using the ID, we can retrieve documents from the database:

```
$ curl -XGET http://127.0.0.1:5984/people/21b5ad83-0ad6-47c7-
86f8-d9636113160a
```

```
{"name":"Rocko Artischocko","likes":["Burritos","Node.
js","Music"],"_id":"21b5ad83-0ad6-47c7-86f8-d9636113160a",
"_rev":"1-411894affa038a6fd7a164e1bfd84146"}
```

Great! You should have a database up and running! If you have trouble, the next section will help you.

Troubleshooting

Sometimes the installation of a database server doesn't go as we want it to. For Windows and Mac users, this section covers how to get a missing curl program. For Linux users, this section solves a typical error related to file watchers on Linux systems.

Getting curl

curl is a command-line client for HTTP requests. It is available for all major operating systems. macOS users can install it by using brew . For Windows, builds are available at http://curl.haxx.se/download.html.

Fixing a File-Watcher Error

On Linux, I got an error because my user already watched too much files:

```
$ npm run start
> theclibook-database@1.0.0 start /home/rocko/clibook/
sourcecode/database
> pouchdb-server --in-memory

fs.js:1236
    throw error;
    ^

Error: watch ./log.txt ENOSPC
    at exports._errnoException (util.js:874:11)
    at FSWatcher.start (fs.js:1234:19)
    at Object.fs.watch (fs.js:1262:11)
    at Tail.watch (/home/rocko/clibook/sourcecode/database/node_
    modules/pouchdb-server/node_modules/tail/tail.js:83:32)
    at new Tail (/home/rocko/clibook/sourcecode/database/node_
    modules/pouchdb-server/node_modules/tail/tail.js:72:10)
    at /home/rocko/clibook/sourcecode/database/node_modules/
    pouchdb-server/lib/logging.js:69:20
    at FSReqWrap.cb [as oncomplete] (fs.js:212:19)

npm ERR! Linux 3.13.0-71-generic
npm ERR! argv "/home/rocko/.nvm/versions/node/v4.2.3/bin/node"
"/home/rocko/.nvm/versions/node/v4.2.3/bin/npm" "run" "start"
npm ERR! node v4.2.3
npm ERR! npm  v3.5.1
npm ERR! code ELIFECYCLE
npm ERR! theclibook-database@1.0.0 start: `pouchdb-server --in-
memory`
npm ERR! Exit status 1
```

```
npm ERR!
npm ERR! Failed at the theclibook-database@1.0.0 start script
'pouchdb-server --in-memory'.
npm ERR! Make sure you have the latest version of node.js and
npm installed.
npm ERR! If you do, this is most likely a problem with the
theclibook-database package,
npm ERR! not with npm itself.
npm ERR! Tell the author that this fails on your system:
npm ERR!      pouchdb-server --in-memory
npm ERR! You can get information on how to open an issue for
this project with:
npm ERR!      npm bugs theclibook-database
npm ERR! Or if that isn't available, you can get their info via:
npm ERR!      npm owner ls theclibook-database
npm ERR! There is likely additional logging output above.

npm ERR! Please include the following file with any support request:
npm ERR!      /home/rocko/clibook/sourcecode/database/npm-debug.log
```

I fixed the problem by raising the file limit via this command:

```
$ echo fs.inotify.max_user_watches=524288 | sudo tee -a /etc/
sysctl.conf && sudo sysctl -p
```

Hopefully, you have a working database server now. The next section focuses on the development of our command-line tool.

Performing a Simple Status Check

Our first command will check whether the database is up and running. Our users can use this command to see whether the database server is running, and we can use the command internally for the commands which require a running database.

The command for checking whether a database server is online looks like this:

```
$ lounger isonline http://192.168.0.1:5984
http://192.168.0.1:5984 is up and running
```

The API looks like this:

```
$ lounger.commands.isonline('http://example.com')
```

It's often helpful to write down a planned command, in order to get a feeling for it. After you have settled on a name and signature for the command, you can start with its development. In this case, we have to start creating our tool from scratch.

Starting from Scratch

To get started, we have to create a package.json file. Luckily, npm provides a nice assistant for creating these files. You can see the finished process in Figure 2-1.

```
$ npm init
```

```
●○○                                    1. bash
(22:35:54) [robert@tequila-new] ~/sourcecode/lounger $ npm init
This utility will walk you through creating a package.json file.
It only covers the most common items, and tries to guess sensible defaults.

See `npm help json` for definitive documentation on these fields
and exactly what they do.

Use `npm install <pkg> --save` afterwards to install a package and
save it as a dependency in the package.json file.

Press ^C at any time to quit.
name: (lounger)
version: (1.0.0)
description: a tool for couchdb/pouchdb administration
entry point: (index.js)
test command: mocha -R spec
git repository:
keywords: couchdb pouchdb
author: Robert Kowalski <rok@kowalski.gd>
license: (ISC)
About to write to /Users/robert/sourcecode/lounger/package.json:

{
  "name": "lounger",
  "version": "1.0.0",
  "description": "a tool for couchdb/pouchdb administration",
  "main": "index.js",
  "scripts": {
    "test": "mocha -R spec"
  },
  "keywords": [
    "couchdb",
    "pouchdb"
  ],
  "author": "Robert Kowalski <rok@kowalski.gd>",
  "license": "ISC"
}

Is this ok? (yes) yes
(22:36:37) [robert@tequila-new] ~/sourcecode/lounger $ ▮
```

Figure 2-1. *The assistant from npm init to create a package.json file*

We then just answer the questions npm asks us.

Additionally, we have to create three folders: test, lib, and bin. The test folder will contain our unit and integration tests, and lib will contain the core of our command-line client. The bin folder will contain a small wrapper that will boot up the core of our client.

CouchDB and PouchDB both return a welcome message when we access the root URL at http://localhost:5984.

```
$ curl localhost:5984
```

CouchDB returns the following:

```
{"couchdb":"Welcome","uuid":"17ed4b2d8923975cf658e20e219faf95",
"version":"1.5.0","vendor":{"version":"14.04","name":"Ubuntu"}}
```

PouchDB returns this:

```
{"express-pouchdb":"Welcome!","version":"1.0.1","vendor":
{"name":"PouchDB authors","version":"1.0.1"},"uuid":
"4fad2c01-ba32-4249-8278-8786e877c397"}
```

We will use this behavior to check whether the database is online.

A Helping Ecosystem

As already mentioned, Node.js has a great ecosystem. It has many battle-proven modules that can help us solve our tasks.

For our status check, we will use the request module to handle our HTTP requests. mocha will run our test suite, and nock will help us mock HTTP responses without having to boot a database instance for the test suite.

The arguments --save and --save-dev will add the packages to the dependencies and devDependencies sections of our package.json file, respectively. The development dependencies are needed just for development, not for running the package in production:

```
$ npm i --save request
$ npm i --save-dev mocha nock
```

After running the commands, we should have everything we need for now.

Choose your own flavors   There are many good test runners for Node.js. Some alternatives to mocha are the npm modules tap, tape, or lab.

My package.json file looks like this now:

```json
{
  "name": "lounger",
  "version": "1.0.0",
  "description": "a tool for couchdb/pouchdb administration",
  "main": "lib/lounger.js",
  "directories": {
    "test": "test"
  },
  "dependencies": {
    "request": "^2.67.0"
  },
  "devDependencies": {
    "mocha": "^2.3.4",
    "nock": "^5.2.1"
  },
  "scripts": {
    "test": "mocha -R spec"
  },
  "keywords": [
    "couchdb",
    "pouchdb"
  ],
  "author": "Robert Kowalski <rok@kowalski.gd>"
}
```

Various development techniques such as test-driven development (TDD) are beyond the scope of this book. But if you are really into TDD, you can write failing tests with mocha before we implement the actual code. A few suggestions:

- Detect whether the database is online.

- Detect offline databases.

- Detect whether something is online, but not a CouchDB/PouchDB database.

- Ensure that only valid URLs are accepted.

Written in mocha and ES6, we get a few failing tests in test/isonline.js:

```
'use strict';

const assert = require('assert');
const nock = require('nock');

describe('isonline', () => {
  it('detects if the database is online', () => {

    assert.equal('foo', 'to implement');
  });

  it('detects offline databases', () => {

    assert.equal('foo', 'to implement');
  });

  it('detects if something is online, but not a CouchDB/
PouchDB', () => {

    assert.equal('foo', 'to implement');
  });
```

```
it('just accepts valid urls', () => {

    assert.equal('foo', 'to implement');
  });
});
```

To run the test suite, we have to type either npm test or npm t on the terminal.

Note   The code for this section can be found at sourcecode/
client-boilerplate.

The Internals of the isonline Command

Let's create and edit the lib/isonline.js file. The file name is important, as we will use it later during the bootstrap of the client. As a first step, we have to require our dependency request:

```
'use strict';

const request = require('request');
```

To make a request, we create the isOnline function, which will take a URL and send the request:

```
function isOnline (url) {
  return new Promise((resolve, reject) => {
    request({
      uri: url,
      json: true
    }, (err, res, body) => {
```

If there is no HTTP service at all listening on the specified URL, we resolve the promise with an object that contains the URL as a key, and false as a value:

```
if (err && (err.code === 'ECONNREFUSED' || err.code ===
'ENOTFOUND')) {
  return resolve({[url]: false});
}
```

For all other errors, we reject the promise:

```
// any other error
if (err) {
  return reject(err);
}
```

If we get a Welcome response from CouchDB or PouchDB, we can safely assume that the database server is online:

```
// maybe we got a welcome from CouchDB / PouchDB
const isDatabase = (body.couchdb === 'Welcome' ||
  body['express-pouchdb'] === 'Welcome!');

return resolve({[url]: isDatabase});
```

As a last step, we have to export the function:

```
exports.api = isOnline;
```

Here is the whole function:

```
function isOnline (url) {
  return new Promise((resolve, reject) => {
    request({
      uri: url,
      json: true
    }, (err, res, body) => {
```

```
      // db is down
      if (err && (err.code === 'ECONNREFUSED' || err.code ===
      'ENOTFOUND')) {
        return resolve({[url]: false});
      }

      // any other error
      if (err) {
        return reject(err);
      }

      // maybe we got a welcome from CouchDB / PouchDB
      const isDatabase = (body.couchdb === 'Welcome' ||
        body['express-pouchdb'] === 'Welcome!');

      return resolve({[url]: isDatabase});
    });
  });
}
exports.api = isOnline;
```

We can try our function on the Node.js REPL:

```
$ node
> const isonline = require('./lib/isonline.js').api;
undefined
> isonline('http://example.com').then(console.log);
Promise { <pending> }
> { 'http://example.com': false }
> isonline('http://doesnotexist.example.com').then(console.log);
Promise { <pending> }
> { 'http://doesnotexist.example.com': false }
> isonline('http://localhost:5984').then(console.log);
```

```
Promise { <pending> }
> { 'http://localhost:5984': true }
```

Congratulations! We just finished the first part, the API for our new command!

The CLI Part

It would be frustrating for end users if that was the command-line interface they had to use. The output is not easily readable, and the functionality is not easy to understand. The API function doesn't print to the console, which is perfect for an API, but not desirable for a CLI. Running the API function even requires some Node.js knowledge. So let's add a nice CLI function to our isonline.js file and export it as cli:

```
function cli (url) {
  return new Promise((resolve, reject) => {

  });
}
exports.cli = cli;
```

Like our other functions, this function returns a promise. We then call isOnline and print the result on stdout for the users who use the command-line client on the terminal:

```
isOnline(url).then((res) => {

  Object.keys(results).forEach((entry) => {
    let msg = 'seems to be offline';
    if (results[entry]) {
      msg = 'seems to be online';
    }
```

```
      // print on stdout for terminal users
      console.log(entry, msg);
      resolve(results);
    });
  });
```

The full code:

```
function cli (url) {
return new Promise((resolve, reject) => {

  isOnline(url).then((res) => {

    Object.keys(results).forEach((entry) => {
      let msg = 'seems to be offline';
      if (results[entry]) {
        msg = 'seems to be online';
      }

      // print on stdout for terminal users
      console.log(entry, msg);
      resolve(results);
    });
  });

  });
}
exports.cli = cli;
```

It is important to note that we export the command for the API as exports.api, while we export the CLI command under the cli property.

Note   The code for this section can be found at sourcecode/the-status-check.

Booting the Tool

Lounger still needs the code that makes it usable on the command line.
It also lacks a comfortable way to run our API commands. Right now, we
have just one command, but we'll add more soon. To make all commands
easy to use, we have to load all available commands into a namespace. The
lib/lounger.js file will take care of that.

The lounger.js file is the heart of our command-line client. We
require the fs module, as we have to list the files that could contain
commmands:

```
'use strict';

const fs = require('fs');
```

We also require package.json and expose the current version of the
module as a property on the lounger object, which will come in handy later:

```
const pkg = require('../package.json');
```

Making Sure Lounger Is Loaded

It makes sense to ensure that lounger was bootstrapped properly,
especially for programmatic use. To keep track of the async bootstrapping
status, we set lounger.loaded to false:

```
const lounger = { loaded: false };
```

We also store the current version of the module:

```
lounger.version = pkg.version;
```

We need a place to store the API and the CLI commands. As the bootstrapping is async, we will throw an error if someone tries to access the exposed functions before the bootstrap is finished:

```
const api = {}, cli = {};

Object.defineProperty(lounger, 'commands', {
  get: () => {
    if (lounger.loaded === false) {
      throw new Error('run lounger.load before');
    }
    return api;
  }
});

Object.defineProperty(lounger, 'cli', {
  get: () => {
    if (lounger.loaded === false) {
      throw new Error('run lounger.load before');
    }
    return cli;
  }
});
```

The custom getter for Object.defineProperty will throw if lounger.loaded is false and we try to access a property on lounger.cli and lounger.api.

It also works for the autocomplete in the Node.js REPL when you try to hit Tab for completion. Just try it!

The last part of the file is the actual bootstrapping, where we get all files in the folder lib and require them if they are JavaScript files and not lounger.js, the file we are currently working with.

The function to bootstrap lounger is called `lounger.load`. In this case, we are using a named function. A named function can be helpful in a stacktrace in case the application crashes:

```
lounger.load = function load () {
  return new Promise((resolve, reject) => {

  });
};
```

The `fs.readdir` function will list all files in a directory. We iterate over the list of files that `fs.readdir` returns:

```
lounger.load = function load () {
  return new Promise((resolve, reject) => {
    fs.readdir(__dirname, (err, files) => {
      files.forEach((file) => {

      });
    });
  });
};
```

If the file is not a JS file or is `lounger.js` itself, we ignore it by returning early:

```
if (!/\.js$/.test(file) || file === 'lounger.js') {
  return;
}
```

In all other cases, we assume that we found a command for lounger. We take everything from the file name before the `.js` and save it as `cmd`:

```
const cmd = file.match(/(.*)\.js$/)[1];
```

We require the file:

```
const mod = require('./' + file);
```

If a file exports an API command as the `api` property, we expose it on `lounger.commands`. All CLI commands are available on `lounger.cli`:

```
if (mod.cli) {
  cli[cmd] = mod.cli;
}

if (mod.api) {
  api[cmd] = mod.api;
}
```

After the `forEach` loop is finished and all commands are loaded, we can set `lounger.loaded` to `true`. This will prevent the checks we added previously from throwing:

```
lounger.loaded = true;
```

As a last step, we resolve the promise:

```
resolve(lounger);
```

The whole `lounger.load` function is shown here:

```
lounger.load = function load () {
  return new Promise((resolve, reject) => {
    fs.readdir(__dirname, (err, files) => {
      files.forEach((file) => {
        if (!/\.js$/.test(file) || file === 'lounger.js') {
          return;
        }

        const cmd = file.match(/(.*)\.js$/)[1];
        const mod = require('./' + file);
```

```
    if (mod.cli) {
      cli[cmd] = mod.cli;
    }

    if (mod.api) {
      api[cmd] = mod.api;
    }

  });
  lounger.loaded = true;
  resolve(lounger);
    });
  });
};
```

We almost forgot to export lounger, so we add module.exports at the end of the file:

```
module.exports = lounger;
```

We can already use the code:

```
$ node
> const lounger = require('./lib/lounger.js'); lounger.load().
then(console.log);
Promise { <pending> }
> { loaded: true, version: '1.0.0', load: [Function: load] }
> lounger.commands
{ isonline: [Function: isOnline] }
> lounger.cli
{ isonline: [Function: cli] }
> lounger.commands.isonline('http://localhost:5984').
then(console.log);
Promise { <pending> }
> { 'http://localhost:5984': true }
```

The last step in this section is to make lounger usable on the terminal itself. For this task, we've already created the `bin` folder. Now it's time to put the file called `lounger-cli.js` into `bin`!

A Nice Way to Interact from the Command Line

npm has a nice feature: if we add a JavaScript file to a property called `bin` in the `package.json` file of a module, npm will add it to our PATH if we are installing the package globally (with `npm install -g lounger`).

If we have the `bin` property defined and lounger is globally installed, it becomes available as `lounger` (which is our package name) on the terminal—quite comfortable! To inform the user that a package is intended to be installed globally, we can add `preferGlobal: true` to `package.json` (see `https://docs.npmjs.com/files/package.json#preferglobal`).

To enable the two features, we add these two lines to our `package.json`:

```
"bin": "./bin/lounger-cli",
"preferGlobal": true,
```

Additionally, we have to make `bin/lounger-cli` executable, if we are on Linux or macOS:

```
$ chmod +x bin/lounger-cli
```

The first line of our `lounger-cli` file will be a *shebang line*. This tells Linxux/Unix shell users that it must run our file with Node.js:

```
#!/usr/bin/env node
```

Afterward, we load `lib/lounger.js`, the core of our command-line tool:

```
const lounger = require('../lib/lounger.js');
```

The next step is to parse our command-line arguments. In this case, we use the nopt module for this purpose (install it with npm i --save nopt). We could parse the arguments on our own, but a battle-proven module like nopt offers a lot more features and is easier to use. We get the passed command by accessing parsed.argv.remain:

```
const nopt = require('nopt');
const parsed = nopt({}, {}, process.argv, 2);

const cmd = parsed.argv.remain.shift();
```

The next step is to boot the client by calling lounger.load, which will bootstrap the client and populate lounger.commands and lounger.cli. After the promise is resolved, we call the command that was passed on the command line:

```
lounger.load().then(() => {

  lounger.cli[cmd]
    .apply(null, parsed.argv.remain)
    .catch((err) => {
      console.error(err);
    });
}).catch((err) => {
  console.error(err);
});
```

As every command returns a promise, we catch errors with catch and then print them to the console.

We can now test our minimalistic command-line client on the command line:

```
$ npm install -g .
$ lounger isonline http://test.example.com
http://test.example.com seems to be offline or no database
```

And given our PouchDB/CouchDB server is running:

```
$ lounger isonline http://localhost:5984
http://localhost:5984 seems to be online
```

Instead of running npm install -g . after each code change, you can run npm link in your module directory. This will link the global installation to the current directory, which means that every change is immediately available, as long as the directory does not change.

Note   The code for this section can be found at sourcecode/client-bootstrap.

Choose your own flavors   There are countless good argument-parsing libraries on npm. Some alternatives to nopt are commander, optimist, and yargs.

Summary

In this chapter, we created the first basic building block for our command-line client. We now have a solid foundation for an extensible command-line client. We also added our first command. Yet we are still far from a product that our users would love and promote. Our CLI still has rough edges and is missing a lot of the features that successful CLIs have. We will fix those issues in the next chapter, where we'll look at at usability and accessibility.

CHAPTER 3

Making Our CLI More Accessible

In the preceding chapter, we built a solid base for our command-line tool. We loaded our first command, and the whole program is executable on the command line. We will now focus on usability and accessibility. We will look at how to improve error handling and provide our users with a guiding hand, even if the program crashes. With JSON support and shorthand, we'll bring a smile to the faces of our power users. We'll also create different formats for our documentation. Before our first production release, we'll add a flexible system for managing configuration.

Error Handling

You already learned that no user enjoys cryptic error messages and stacktraces. Sadly, that is still the case for our lounger application. Making the application more accessible should be our first priority.

Right now, lounger doesn't do anything about wrong input for the `isonline` command:

```
$ lounger isonline ragrragr
$
```

© Robert Kowalski 2017
R. Kowalski, *The CLI Book*, https://doi.org/10.1007/978-1-4842-3177-7_3

Another caveat to consider is, are we handling errors correctly so people can use the command-line client in their bash scripts?

```
$ lounger isonline ragrragr
$ echo $?
0
```

Wouldn't it be nicer to give users a hint about the correct usage of the program right away, without opening any documentation? Nobody enjoys sitting in front of a black terminal, having no idea what to do. While we are at it, we can also fix the wrong exit code, which is currently signaling a successfully executed program.

Why isn't our `console.error` call in `bin/lounger-cli` printing anything? It turns out that we introduced a subtle bug: we forgot the `.catch` for our promise-returning call in `lib/isonline.js`. Given that the API function `isOnline` rejects the promise, we have no handler in the `cli` function to take care of it. No problem—we'll add the `.catch` right now:

```
function cli (url) {
  return new Promise((resolve, reject) => {

    isOnline(url).then((results) => {

      // print on stdout for terminal users
      Object.keys(results).forEach((entry) => {
        let msg = 'seems to be offline or no database server';
        if (results[entry]) {
          msg = 'seems to be online';
        }

        console.log(entry, msg);
        resolve(results);
      });
```

```
    }).catch(reject);  // add the missing catch
  });
}
exports.cli = cli;
```

Our next try is a bit more successful:

```
$ lounger isonline ragrragr
[Error: Invalid URI "ragrragr"]
```

Not sure if you are happy with it? I'm not! Just imagine someone who has never used Node.js or the terminal, or maybe even someone who is completely new to computers. The Invalid URI message won't help them much to get their task done. Twenty years ago, they would have had to get a book from the library in order to find out what a URI is, and today they would have to search Google for it. Instead, they could have fun with our CLI and get things done! In the next section, we will take a look at how to improve error messages that originate from wrong input.

Handling Usage Errors

Usage errors comprise everything related to wrong usage of the interface. Usually, it's wrong input that's causing trouble. Often the argument order is switched by accident. Fortunately, we can fix this issue by adding validations for the arguments in isonline.js.

If the user does not provide a URL to the CLI, we'll have a new error with the message Usage: lounger isonline <url>, which describes how the user should use the command. We set the type of the error to EUSAGE, which will be important later. In lounger, all errors that are thrown because the user provided the wrong input get the type EUSAGE. All other cases related to bugs don't get the type EUSAGE:

```
function cli (url) {
  return new Promise((resolve, reject) => {
```

```
if (!url) {
  const err = new Error('Usage: lounger isonline <url>');
  err.type = 'EUSAGE';
  return reject(err);
}
```

The less-than sign and greater-than sign around url indicate that it is a required argument and not optional. The last command in the block rejects the promise with our error and returns, in order to prevent the execution of the following code.

Tip   Early returns are useful for reducing cyclomatic complexity. *Cyclomatic complexity* is a measurement of the complexity of code. For example, code appears more complex when if and else blocks are nested, as these nested blocks make it harder for the human brain to reason about the flow of the program's execution.

Additionally. we have to check whether the URL is valid:

```
if (!/^(http:|https:)/.test(url)) {
  const err = new Error([
    'invalid protocol, must be https or http',
    'Usage: lounger isonline <url>'
  ].join('\n'));
  err.type = 'EUSAGE';
  return reject(err);
}
```

In this case, we set the error type to EUSAGE again and reject the promise. Additionally, we tell the user that we expect a valid URL with a protocol that is usable for us.

On our next try, we will get a slightly better result:

```
$ ./bin/lounger-cli isonline dsf
{ [Error: invalid protocol, must be https or http
Usage: lounger isonline <url>] type: 'EUSAGE' }
```

As we reject the promise, the console.error that we added in bin/lounger-cli prints the error object. By adding a few lines of code, we can format it so humans can read it better. We will install the npmlog logger for it (hint: npm i is short for npm install):

```
$ npm i --save npmlog
```

We require the logger at the top of bin/lounger-cli, the file where we catch the rejected promise:

```
const log = require('npmlog');
```

Next, we add the errorHandler function to bin/lounger-cli. If the error is a usage error (of type EUSAGE), we log the message and exit with error code 1. All other errors are logged using log.error(err) for now:

```
function errorHandler (err) {
  if (!err) {
    process.exit(1);
  }

  if (err.type === 'EUSAGE') {
    err.message && log.error(err.message);
    process.exit(1);
  }

  log.error(err);
  process.exit(1);
}
```

Now we have to switch from the old `console.error` call to our new error-handling function:

```
lounger.load().then(() => {

  lounger.cli[cmd]
    .apply(null, parsed.argv.remain)
    .catch(errorHandler);

}).catch(errorHandler);
```

Cool—let's see if it works:

```
$ lounger isonline
ERR! Usage: lounger isonline <url>
$ echo $?
1
```

Figure 3-1 shows the result. That looks a lot better!

Figure 3-1. *A usage error resulting from providing the wrong input to the CLI*

Providing Further Guidance

We still haven't dealt with other errors: errors from dependencies we use, or evil bugs that sneak in, like reference errors. To simulate such an error, we can add a call to a nonexistent function in the `cli` function:

```
function cli (url) {
  return new Promise((resolve, reject) => {
    doesNotExist();
```

If we now run the command-line client, we get this:

```
$ lounger isonline http://example.com
ERR! ReferenceError: doesNotExist is not defined
```

If I had just downloaded the command-line client and tried to use it, I would be quite puzzled. Say I started a new job and tried to use the same tool that my coworkers were using, but downloaded a newer release with bugs. I would be stuck, with no further information about how to continue. To be honest, if I hadn't programmed in JavaScript for years, this stacktrace would really puzzle me!

Most people would just stop using our program and switch to an alternative. Very few would go on a journey of finding out where to submit an issue or even write a PR. Usually, computers are frustrating, and people don't want to spend multiple hours trying to find someone to help them with a cryptic message. So how about making this process as easy as possible, reducing the friction where we can?

npm itself supports a `bugs` property in `package.json`. If we add the following to the `package.json` file of lounger, a call to `npm  bugs` will open `http://example.com/lounger/issues` in a browser for us:

```
"bugs": {
  "url": "http://example.com/lounger/issues"
},
```

Cool—we have a central place for storing the URL to our issue tracker. We can also add the URL to our stacktraces, in order to make submitting bugs for our users easier. We need to require `package.json` in `bin/lounger-cli`, the file where we print our errors anyway:

```
const pkg = require('./package.json');
```

By altering our errorHandler, we make it print full stacktraces.
Additionally, we ask the user to open an issue, as it is pretty clear right now
that the error was not a usage error that was caught by our validations:

```
function errorHandler (err) {
  if (!err) {
    process.exit(1);
  }

  if (err.type === 'EUSAGE') {
    err.message && log.error(err.message);
    process.exit(1);
  }

  err.message && log.error(err.message);

  if (err.stack) {
    log.error('', err.stack);
    log.error('', '');
    log.error('', '');
    log.error('', 'lounger:', pkg.version, 'node:', process.
    version);
    log.error('', 'please open an issue including this log on '
    + pkg.bugs.url);
  }
  process.exit(1);
}
```

OK, here's the next try:

```
$ lounger isonline http://example.com
ERR! doesNotExist is not defined
ERR! ReferenceError: doesNotExist is not defined
ERR!     at /home/rocko/clibook/sourcecode/error-handling/lib/
         isonline.js:35:7
```

```
ERR!     at cli (/home/rocko/clibook/sourcecode/error-handling/
         lib/isonline.js:34:10)
ERR!     at /home/rocko/clibook/sourcecode/error-handling/bin/
         lounger-cli:15:6
ERR!
ERR!
ERR! lounger: 1.0.0 node: v9.1.0
ERR! please open an issue including this log on http://example.
     com/lounger/issues
```

Awesome! The stacktrace with line numbers is useful for us. The current version of the program and the Node.js environment help us, too. In case the command-line client really hits a wall, we receive a lot of information in order to debug the process. Even more important: the user gets all the information needed to create an issue. We remove a lot of friction from the process by directly pointing to the issue tracker and providing all information that is needed to describe the bug—no long back and forth about the current Node version or the missing logfile!

Note   The code for this section can be found at `sourcecode/error-handling`.

JSON Support and Shorthand

JSON support is useful for all users who want to take the output from the CLI and process it programatically with their own tools. By adding a `--json` flag to our `isonline` command, we can add this useful feature with a few lines of code. We have to tell our argument parser about it; in this case, we are telling nopt that we want to have `--json` handled as a Boolean in `bin/lounger-cli`:

```
const parsed = nopt({
  'json': [Boolean]
}, {'j': '--json'}, process.argv, 2);
```

Based on the type `Boolean,` nopt will automatically also add
`--no-json` for us, which will come in handy when we add additional
configuration by file later. Additionally, we register a shorthand option for
our power users: they can use `-j` instead of `--json`.

We then pass the result `parsed` into `lounger.load`:

```
const parsed = nopt({
  'json': [Boolean]
}, {'j': '--json'}, process.argv, 2);

const cmd = parsed.argv.remain.shift();

lounger.load(parsed).then(() => {

  lounger.cli[cmd]
    .apply(null, parsed.argv.remain)
    .catch(errorHandler);

}).catch(errorHandler);
```

`longer.load` adds a `lounger.config.get` command and makes it
available for us as part of the bootstrap:

```
lounger.load = function load (opts) {
  return new Promise((resolve, reject) => {

    lounger.config = {
      get: (key) => {
        return opts[key];
      }
    };

    fs.readdir(__dirname, (err, files) => {
```

We require `lounger.js` in our `isonline.js` file:

```
const lounger = require('./lounger.js');
```

As a last step, we the check for `json-flag` in our `cli` function after we get the results back:

```
isOnline(url).then((results) => {

  if (lounger.config.get('json')) {
    console.log(results);
    resolve(results);
    return;
  }
```

That's it! We can test the command:

```
$ lounger isonline http://example.com
http://example.com seems to be offline or no database server

$ lounger isonline http://example.com --json
{ 'http://example.com': false }

$ lounger isonline http://example.com -j
{ 'http://example.com': false }
```

Our users can now pipe the output on their terminals into other consumers and process the results. We also added our first command-line flag to lounger to modify the execution of a command. Great!

Note   The code and tests for this section are in `sourcecode/json-flags`.

Documentation

The last step to finish our `isonline` command is to add proper documentation. We will write this documentation in Markdown. We need documentation for the API and CLI commands. The API docs will live in `doc/api`, and the CLI commands will live in `doc/cli`. I know that most programmers hate writing documentation, but it will help us a lot: new users will be able to get up and running easier, and we won't lose them before they had the chance to enjoy our product. Additionally, we make our lives easier by documenting the functionality once, so people don't have to open issues or ask in a chat how they can use a command. It's a win-win situation. We start with `doc/api/lounger-isonline.md`, which describes the API that is available at `lounger.commands`:

```
lounger-isonline(3) -- check if a database is online
====================================================
```

The heading describes our command as `lounger-isonline(3)` and then adds a short explanation of what the command is about. The number in parentheses describes the type of the section. For a man page, a library function is noted by a `3`, and a user command would be a `1` (spoiler: our CLI command is a user command).

The next section describes how our users can use the command:

```
## SYNOPSIS

    lounger.commands.isonline(url)
```

The last part is a detailed description of how the command works:

```
## DESCRIPTION

Check if a CouchDB / PouchDB database is available on the current
network.
```

url:
The url must be a `String` and must be a url using the http or https
protocol.

The command returns a promise. The promise returns an Object.
The key of the Object is the provided url and the values are of
type `Boolean`.
`true` indicates an online CouchDB / PouchDB node.

That's it for the API part. We can now add the text for doc/cli/
lounger-isonline.md:

```
lounger-isonline(1) -- check if a database is online
=====================================================

    lounger isonline <url> [--json]

## DESCRIPTION

  <url>:
Check if a database node is currently online or available.

`isonline` prints the result as human readable output. JSON
output is also supported by passing the `--json` flag.
```

With the small 1 in lounger-isonline(1), we are signaling that this
help section explains a user command. The less-than and greater-than
symbols in <url> show the user that url is a mandatory argument; without
it, the command won't work. The square brackets of [--json] mean that
the --json flag is an *optional* command. With our first documentation
pages ready, we can move to the next section and render it into various
output formats.

Rendering the Documentation

Now that we have the sources for our documentation, we can start to build our documentation from our sources with `marked` and `marked-man`:

```
$ npm i --save-dev marked marked-man
```

A makefile would be a great fit for generating the documentation from the source. Sadly, it is hard to get makefiles to work on Windows, so we will write our build steps in JavaScript. In the root directory of lounger, we create the file `build.js`. Additionally, we have to install `mkdirp` and `rimraf`; `mkdirp` provides the functionality we know from the Linux command `mkdir -p` in a cross-platform way: it creates directories and subdirectories recursively. The `rimraf` module brings us the equivalent of `rm -rf` to the Node.js platform: deleting directories recursively. We also will use the `glob` module to match all needed files for our documentation build:

```
$ npm i --save-dev mkdirp rimraf glob
```

Our first function will be a function to clean a fresh folder structure where we can save our man pages:

```
'use strict';

const mkdirp = require('mkdirp');
const rimraf = require('rimraf');
const glob = require('glob');
const path = require('path');

function cleanUpMan () {
  rimraf.sync(__dirname + '/man/');
  // re-create the target directory
  mkdirp.sync(__dirname + '/man/');
}
```

We have to find out which Markdown files are available for the compile. Our sources for documentation are at doc/api or at doc/cli. Additionally, we will have some content in doc/website that is specific to the web site (the content for index.html).

The getSources function helps us to get the full path to the Markdown files for each type of source (api, doc, website). It returns the relative path of the matching glob and then uses the path.resolve function to get the full path in a cross-platform way.

```
function getSources (type) {
  const files = glob.sync('doc/' + type + '/*.md');

  return files.map(file => path.resolve(file));
}
```

The sources object stores an array of the found files for each type:

```
const sources = {
  api: getSources('api'),
  cli: getSources('cli'),
  websiteIndex: getSources('website'),
};
```

We can clean up our target directory now and get a list of file names that we want to convert. We still need to find out the target path and file name for the converted files. Man pages have different file endings, depending on the kind of functionality they describe. Our man pages for the CLI would get the ending .1 (user commands), and our API function would get the ending .3 (library functions). We also have to change /doc/cli/ and /doc/api/ in the path of the file to our target directory, /man/. We have to take special care of the path separators. On Windows, the separators are \\ instead of /. That means the path doc/api becomes doc\\api on Windows. The good news is that we can access the current path separator by using path.sep in Node.js (the separator is provided by the core module path):

```
function getTargetForManpages (currentFile, type) {
  let target;
  // set the right section for the man page on unix systems

  if (type === 'cli') {
    target = currentFile.replace(/\.md$/, '.1');
  }

  if (type === 'api') {
    target = currentFile.replace(/\.md$/, '.3');
  }

  // replace the source dir with the target dir
  // do it for the windows path (doc\\api) and the unix path
  (doc/api)
  target = target
    .replace(['doc', 'cli'].join(path.sep), 'man')
    .replace(['doc', 'api'].join(path.sep), 'man');

  return target;
}
```

Right now, we just want to create man pages from our documents in
the api and cli folders.

Based on these building blocks, we can create the final buildMan
function that will finally build our man pages. It will make use of the
functions we just created and spawn a child process that compiles the
Markdown files by using marked-man. We will use the spawnSync function
from the Node core to spawn the processes. As we write the result to the
file system, we have to require the fs module, too:

```
const fs = require('fs');
const spawnSync = require('child_process').spawnSync;
```

The first job is cleaning up to get a new target directory without any files from previous builds. We then iterate over our sources and get the target for our new generated file. The file is then written to the hard disk by using fs.writeFileSync. We stop the execution of the web-site index, as we don't want to do use it for a man page right now. In the next iteration, we could definitely add a main page for the lounger man pages:

```
function buildMan () {
  cleanUpMan();

  Object.keys(sources).forEach(type => {

    sources[type].forEach(currentFile => {

      if (type === 'websiteIndex') {
        return;
      }

      // convert markdown to man-pages
      const out = spawnSync('node', [
        './node_modules/marked-man/bin/marked-man',
        currentFile
      ]);

      const target = getTargetForManpages(currentFile, type);

      // write output to target file
      fs.writeFileSync(target, out.stdout, 'utf8');
    })
  });
}
buildMan();
```

With `buildMan();` in the last line, we kick off the build process every time we run the script with Node. A few modifications to our `package.json` could make it an npm script and run the build before a publish, so our users don't have to compile anything on their own as part of the installation. This ensures that every user really gets the same content of the package and makes installations faster.

In `package.json,` we modify the `scripts` section and add entries for `build` and `prepublishOnly`. The `prepublishOnly` entry is a special hook for npm. It will run every time before we publish the package to the registry:

```
"scripts": {
  "test": "mocha -R spec",
  "docs": "node ./build",
  "prepublishOnly": "npm run docs"
},
```

Since npm version 5 `prepublish` is deprecated. It still works, but for build steps it is advised to use prepublishOnly or prepare instead.

npm also offers a nice feature for man pages: npm can install them for the user so they are available on the terminal via `man <command>` for Linux/Unix users. In order to do that, we have to add another entry to our `package.json`, the `man` entry in the `directories` section:

```
"directories": {
  "man": "./man"
},
```

The entry points to our local man-pages directory. If you are on Unix/Linux, you can see if the man pages work now:

```
$ npm run docs

> lounger@1.0.0 docs /home/rocko/clibook/sourcecode/documentation
> node ./build
```

```
$ npm install -g .

> lounger@1.0.0 prepublish /home/rocko/clibook/sourcecode/
documentation

> npm run docs

> lounger@1.0.0 docs /home/rocko/clibook/sourcecode/
documentation
> node ./build

/home/rocko/.nvm/versions/node/v9.1.0/bin/lounger -> /home/
rocko/.nvm/versions/node/v9.1.0/lib/node_modules/lounger/bin/
lounger-cli
/home/rocko/.nvm/versions/node/v9.1.0/lib
└── lounger@1.0.0
```

We can now type in the command to show a man page, which will displayonscreen (Figure 3-2):

```
$ man lounger-isonline
```

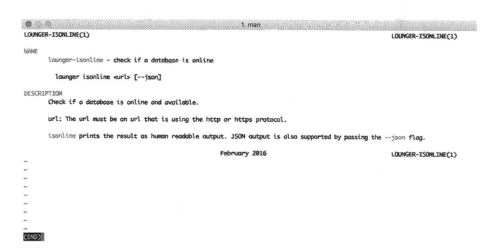

Figure 3-2. *The man page for lounger, our command-line client*

It is also possible to select a specific section:

```
$ man 3 lounger-isonline
$ man 1 lounger-isonline
```

With the man pages ready to ship, we can focus on the HTML output.

Providing HTML Output

For our HTML-based documentation, we have to add the HTML-specific part now. We'll create a folder called website in the doc folder of our module. It will contain the templates for the web site that are used to "frame" the document output.

In the website folder, we put a template.html file with some basic markup, and most important, placeholders!

```
<!doctype html>
<html lang="en">
<head>
  <meta charset="utf-8">
  <title>The lounger manual & documentation</title>
</head>
<body>

  <div class="wrapper">
    <a href="./">lounger</a>

    <div class="content">
      __CONTENT__
    </div>
  </div>
  <nav class="toc-container">
    <div class="toc main-toc">
```

```
      __TOC__
    </div>
  </nav>

</body>
</html>
```

We need to create some content for the root of our website to welcome the user. I will provide a very short example. In general, the landing page should give the user an idea of what the command-line client is about and maybe also demo it. A screencast is a great way to demonstrate some of the core features. For some inspiration on what to put on the site, feel free to visit http://apache.github.io/couchdb-nmo, which is the page for the command-line client I wrote. Next to our template in doc/website we add the bespoke index page as index.md:

```
# Welcome to Lounger

Lounger is a friendly administration tool for CouchDB and PouchDB.

```
# you will need Node.js > 8 for lounger
npm install -g lounger
```

Things you can do with lounger:

```
# check if a CouchDB / PouchDB instance is online

lounger isonline http://example.com

```
```

The page is minimalistic but gives a brief overview of what lounger is about. It also shows how our visitors can install it and gives a hint that they need Node.js—not everyone has Node.js installed, and some people may have never heard of npm. Remember: our goal is to make everything as easy as possible for new users, so they never get stuck. In the next section, we are going to implement the required functionality to render our Markdown.

Extending the Build Script

In order to build the web site, we have to add code to build.js. We start by adding another cleanup function for our web-site files, so we can start with a blank slate every time:

```
function cleanUpWebsite () {
  rimraf.sync(__dirname + '/website/');
  mkdirp.sync(__dirname + '/website/');
}
```

Our web site has different targets than the man pages. We add a new function, getTargetForWebsite. Currently, our Markdown files are prefixed with lounger-, which comes in handy for the man pages, but is not very useful for our web site. Instead, we want to prefix files with their type; an API document, for example, would have the prefix api-. This way, we can put pages for the API next to the ones for the CLI, which makes linking easier. The first lines of the getTargetForWebsite function will take care of that task and replace the lounger- prefix with a type-specific prefix. After we replace the prefix, we set the file ending from .md to .html. The final target folder for our compiled results will be ./website, so we have to take care that the directories are set up right. The difference with getTargetForManpages is that we use the website folder instead of man and that we also take care of the path for the doc/website/index.md file:

```
function getTargetForWebsite (currentFile, type) {
  let target = currentFile;
  // modify the filename a bit for our html file:
  // prefix all cli functions with cli- instead of lounger-
  // prefix all api functions with api- instead of lounger-
  if (type === 'cli') {
    target = currentFile.replace(/lounger-/, 'cli-');
  }

  if (type === 'api') {
    target = currentFile.replace(/lounger-/, 'api-');
  }

  // set the file ending to html
  target = target.replace(/\.md$/, '.html');

  // replace the source dir with the target dir
  target = target
    .replace(['doc', 'cli'].join(path.sep), 'website')
    .replace(['doc', 'api'].join(path.sep), 'website')
    .replace(['doc', 'website'].join(path.sep), 'website');

  return target;
}
```

The last item that is missing for our web site is something like a table of contents. getTocForWebsite will create a listing of our API and CLI functions. Later we will insert the table of contents into the TOC placeholder of the template.

The TOC itself gets a nested list of the files we compile. In the future, it might make sense to replace the whole system with a template engine such as Handlebars, Jade, or Nunjucks. I could definitely write a second book about static web-site generation, plus the numerous possible toolchains, but I'm trying to keep it simple for now and just use plain ES6 templates.

After starting an unordered list with `<ul>`, we iterate over the types of our sources again. The files of our `websiteIndex` type are unwanted, and we return early in their case. For all others, we take the type of each section and use it as the first list element. It shows the type of each section (API or CLI) and acts as a heading.

After we get a heading, we iterate over each file from the current section. As the link text differs a bit from the actual hyperlink, we create a constant called `file` and an additional `linktext` constant. For both, we must get rid of the `lounger-` prefix. To create the reference that is used as `href`, we must change the `.md` to an `.html` ending. The link text should not have a file ending at all, so we remove its `.md` ending:

```
function getTocForWebsite () {
  let toc = '<ul>';

  Object.keys(sources).forEach(type => {

    // we don't want the index in our toc for now
    if (type === 'websiteIndex') {
      return;
    }

    toc += `<li><span>${type}</span><ul>`;

    sources[type].forEach(currentFile => {
      const prefix = type === 'cli' ? 'cli-' : 'api-';

      const file = path.basename(currentFile)
        .replace('lounger-', prefix)
        .replace(/\.md/, '.html');

      const linktext = path.basename(currentFile)
        .replace('lounger-', '')
        .replace(/\.md/, '');
```

```
    toc += `<li><a href="${file}">${linktext}</a></li>`;
  });
  toc += '</ul></li>';
});

toc += '</ul>';

return toc;
}
```

We can now take the small functions we created and create the main build function, buildWebsite, from them. The templateFile constant describes where we can find our template file, template.html, which we created at the beginning:

```
const templateFile = __dirname + '/doc/website/template.html';
```

The next step is to replace the placeholders in the templates with the generated table of contents and the different content for each API or CLI method.

In buildWebsite, we call cleanUpWebsite to remove any outdated files as a first step. We read the template with fs.readFileSync and get the table of contents. We then iterate over our sources. This time, we don't spawn a child process with marked-man; we just use marked, which outputs HTML. After we get the target for the current file of the web site, we replace the CONTENT placeholder with it. TOC gets replaced with the table of contents, which is saved in toc at the top of the main function. Moving the read operation of the template and the creation of the TOC out of the loops improves the performance of our build, as we don't have to call them for every new file. The rendered content finally gets written to the disk by using fs.writeFileSync again. The last line in the code snippet finally calls buildWebsite in order to build our web site when we run build.js:

```
function buildWebsite () {
  cleanUpWebsite();

  const template = fs.readFileSync(templateFile, 'utf8');
  const toc = getTocForWebsite();

  Object.keys(sources).forEach(type => {

    sources[type].forEach(currentFile => {

        // convert markdown to website content
      const out = spawnSync('node', [
        './node_modules/marked/bin/marked',
        currentFile
      ]);

      const target = getTargetForWebsite(currentFile, type);

      const rendered = template
        .replace('__CONTENT__', out.stdout)
        .replace('__TOC__', toc);

      // write output to target file
      fs.writeFileSync(target, rendered, 'utf8');
    });
  });
}

buildWebsite();
```

We can now run our build again and take a look at our web site, shown in Figure 3-3, which appears in the website folder:

```
$ npm run docs
```

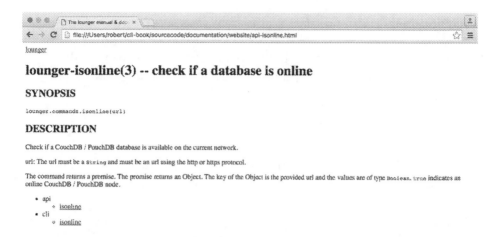

Figure 3-3. *The minimal website for lounger generated from our Markdown*

The site is still missing some content as well as a nice stylesheet. As I already mentioned, building web sites is a topic for a whole new book, and I want to leave it like this for now. Feel free to add more content and styles to the web site. Nevertheless, we just created something that we can deploy to GitHub pages or any other hoster. The best thing about it is that we can ship it with our command-line client as additional documentation for everyone who can't use or doesn't like man pages. We will use both types of documentation in our next section when we create a help system.

Note   The code for this section can be found at `sourcecode/`
`documentation`.

More Help

We have some documentation, but lounger still has some rough edges. If users try to access a command that does not exist, they won't get any advice on how to continue:

```
$ lounger foobar
```

A user who calls lounger with no arguments at all also doesn't get support:

```
$ lounger
```

What's missing is a help page that explains how our users can get their tasks done. It would be awesome if they could open our documentation (web pages or man pages) right from the terminal. Our users shouldn't have to care about man pages or have to find out where we host our web site. The desired behavior of lounger is as follows:

1. The CLI prints a general help message if it was called without a command or if a passed command doesn't exist. This message gives the user a hint on how to proceed further to get the task done.

2. It is easy to get additional help for a command.

This way, we offer help where the user needs it. No need to switch over to Google and search for help. In next two sections, we add the required functionality to lounger.

General Help with a List of Commands

To add the general help screen, we start by creating a new library function, lib/help.js. The first function will print some friendly help text to the user. The help text gets constructed in a helper function (no pun intended).

We can get all of our available commands by calling `Object.keys(lounger.cli)`. We chain a `.join(', ')` call to separate each command with a comma and a space:

```
const lounger = require('./lounger.js');

function getGeneralHelpMessage () {
  const commands = Object.keys(lounger.cli).join(', ');
```

The next part is a template string that explains how to use lounger. We add all available commands that are exposed on the command-line interface. We also explain that users without a clue can run `lounger help` together with the command they are interested in to get detailed help for a command. We also provide an example of how to call the help.

The final line indicates which version of lounger the user is running, which comes in handy in various situations. Usually, people forget which version of a package they have installed. Imagine a user who just read a blog article about lounger version 2.3, which has a great new feature to try. The user installed lounger some time ago, and, sadly, the command is available only since version 2.3 (which was released three days ago). In this case, the user can get immediate feedback that an older version is running.

Here is the whole `getGeneralHelpMessage` function:

```
function getGeneralHelpMessage () {
  const commands = Object.keys(lounger.cli).join(', ');

  const message = `Usage: lounger <command>
```

The available commands for lounger are:

```
${commands}
```

You can get more help on each command with: lounger help
<command>

Example:
lounger help isonline

lounger v${lounger.version} on Node.js ${process.version}`;

  return message;
}

That's already it for the general help message. Next, we are going to extend the help system further.

Help for Each Command

A simple system for accessing help for each command in our command-line client is invaluable. The next function we'll build will try to open the man page if possible. It will fall back to the web site version for Windows users.

The opener module does a great job opening files on different operating systems. This also applies to HTML files, as we want to open them in the default browser of the current operating system. So we install opener as our next dependency:

```
$ npm install --save opener
```

We then require opener at the top of help.js:

```
const opener = require('opener');
```

We also have to spawn the man command later and find out the absolute path for our web-site files:

```
const spawnSync = require('child_process').spawnSync;
const path = require('path');
```

The core module os can help us find out if we are running on Windows:

```
const isWindows = require('os').platform() === 'win32';
```

We then have to spawn the man command or open the default browser for the desired functionality. With stdio: inherit for the spawn command, we can see and interact with the output of the spawned process:

```
function openDocumentation (command) {

  if (isWindows) {
    const htmlFile = path.resolve(__dirname + '/../website/cli-
    ' + command + '.html');
    return opener('file:///' + htmlFile);
 }

  spawnSync('man', ['lounger-' + command], {stdio: 'inherit'});
}
```

The last task is putting all our helper functions together. If a command is not available, we print the general help. If the command exists, we open the man page or the browser, depending on the operating system:

```
exports.cli = help;
function help (command) {
  return new Promise((resolve, reject) => {

    if (!lounger.cli[command]) {
      console.log(getGeneralHelpMessage());
    } else {
      openDocumentation(command);
    }

    resolve();
  });
}
```

If you want, you can also add code to enable the user to configure the type of documentation that is opened. Maybe Linux users prefer the website version of the docs. We can already try the new help command, as it gets picked up by our lounger.js file (Figure 3-4).

Figure 3-4. *Our help command in action*

Our final task in this section is to make sure to print general help when the user does not enter a command at all. In bin/lounger-cli, we require the help.js file and modify the lounger.load call. In case we don't find the command in lounger.cli, we print the general help:

```
const help = require('../lib/help.js');
lounger.load(parsed).then(() => {

  if (!lounger.cli[cmd]) {
    return help.cli();
  }

  lounger.cli[cmd]
    .apply(null, parsed.argv.remain)
    .catch(errorHandler);

}).catch(errorHandler);
```

Congrats! We are finished with the help system now and have made significant progress! Feel free to play around with our new help system by entering these commands:

```
$ lounger blerg
$ lounger
$ lounger help
$ lounger help isonline
```

Note   The code for this section is located at `sourcecode/help-system`.

Configuration

Requiring our users to add their favorite settings as flags by hand every time they use lounger can be cumbersome. A configuration file enables our users to save the settings they need every day. It would be nice if we could support this feature to make our power users happier.

Creating the Configuration File

It is common practice to put the configuration files for command-line tools into the home directory of the user. The home directory is different for every operating system, but the `osenv` module can help us find the current home directory:

```
$ npm install --save osenv
```

We have to see whether a `loungerrc` configuration exists in our home directory, and if not, we have to create an empty one. We do that in `lounger-cli`, in order to keep the API functions free of the side effect. This is the changed `lounger-cli` file, where we added a `require` call for `osenv` and created a configuration file right after the argument parsing. We also add the path to the config file to our parsed arguments:

```
#!/usr/bin/env node

const lounger = require('../lib/lounger.js');
const pkg = require('../package.json');
const log = require('npmlog');
const nopt = require('nopt');
const help = require('../lib/help.js');
const osenv = require('osenv');
const fs = require('fs');

const parsed = nopt({
  'json': [Boolean]
}, {'j': '--json'}, process.argv, 2);

const home = osenv.home();
parsed.loungerconf = home + '/' + '.loungerrc';

if (!fs.existsSync(parsed.loungerconf)) {
  fs.writeFileSync(parsed.loungerconf, '');
}
```

The Heart of Our Configuration System

The config itself will use ini-formatted config files in order to store and read settings. The `config-chain` module loads configurations with different priorities based on the order we load them. It also supports ini-formatted files.

Let's create a lib/config.js file and require config-chain:

```
$ npm i --save config-chain
'use strict';

const cc = require('config-chain');
```

config-chain is able to manage multiple configurations. It will
override configuration settings according to the order we load them.

For our use case, we want the options provided as arguments on the
command line to have the highest priority. They should override the options
from the config file. As the loading of the file is done asynchronously, we
have to listen to the load event emitted by config-chain after it is finished.
For programmatic use of lounger with loungr.load and the API functions no
file based configuration is needed. In those cases we don't try to load the
file. On all errors, we reject our promise and pass the error object:

```
exports.loadConfig = loadConfig;
function loadConfig (nopts) {
  return new Promise((resolve, reject) => {
    let cfg;

    if (!nopts.loungerconf) {
      cfg = cc(nopts)
        .on('load', () => {
          resolve(cfg);
        }).on('error', reject);
    } else {
      cfg = cc(nopts)
        .addFile(nopts.loungerconf, 'ini', 'config')
        .on('load', () => {
          resolve(cfg);
        }).on('error', reject);
    }
  });
};
```

The config object that is returned from `config-chain` has nice get and set methods. We can even save the config back to the configuration file after changing the config by using the save method. For now, we have to integrate `loadConfig` into the bootstrap of lounger. Do you remember the `config.get` method in `lounger.js` from the previous chapter? We will replace it with the config object that is returned by our `load` function.

First, we have to load our config in `lounger.js`:

```
const config = require('./config.js');
```

In `lounger.load`, we are going to load the config:

```
lounger.load = function load (opts) {
  return new Promise((resolve, reject) => {
    config
      .loadConfig(opts)
      .then((cfg) => {

    });
```

The other content of `lounger.load`, including the `fs.readdir` call, is moved into the callback of the chained `then` function:

```
lounger.load = function load (opts) {
  return new Promise((resolve, reject) => {

    config.loadConfig(opts)
      .then((cfg) => {

        lounger.config = cfg;

        fs.readdir(__dirname, (err, files) => {
          files.forEach((file) => {
            if (!/\.js$/.test(file) || file === 'lounger.js') {
              return;
            }
```

```
      const cmd = file.match(/(.*)\.js$/)[1];
      const mod = require('./' + file);
      if (mod.cli) {
        cli[cmd] = mod.cli;
      }

      if (mod.api) {
        api[cmd] = mod.api;
      }

    });
    lounger.loaded = true;
    resolve(lounger);
  });
}).catch(reject);

  });
};
```

If we now run lounger, it will create a config file for us in our home directory. On macOS my config is at ~/.loungerrc.

After the file is created (don't forget to run lounger at least one time), we can set JSON output to true in ~/.loungerrc:

```
json = true
```

Just try out lounger isonline http://example.com, and lounger will print JSON now. We can still override the config on the command line:

```
$ lounger isonline --no-json
```

A Helper to Edit the Configuration

Because manually editing ~/.loungerrc is not very user-friendly, we will build a lounger config command. This command should be used to show the config and its values and to set config values.

Here is the proposed CLI:

```
$ lounger config set json true
$ lounger config get json
```

The API could look like this:

```
lounger.commands.set('json', true)
lounger.commands.get('json')
```

config-chain offers the data provided in the loaded config file as .sources.config.data. For JSON formatted output, we return the whole config if no key is provided:

```
const data = lounger.config.sources.config.data;

if (lounger.config.get('json') && !key) {
  resolve(data);
  return;
}
```

If a key is provided, we build a JSON object that contains only the value for our key:

```
if (lounger.config.get('json') && key) {
  resolve({[key]: data[key]});
  return;
}
```

Given that we don't want JSON formatted output and did provide a key, we return the value:

```
if (key) {
  resolve(lounger.config.sources.config.data[key]);
  return;
}
```

In the last case, where the json setting is set to false, and no key was provided, we simply read the unparsed ini file:

```
resolve(fs.readFileSync(lounger.config.sources));
```

Here is the whole get function:

```
function get (key) {
  return new Promise((resolve, reject) => {
    const data = lounger.config.sources.config.data;

    if (lounger.config.get('json') && !key) {
      resolve(data);
      return;
    }
    if (lounger.config.get('json') && key) {
      resolve({[key]: data[key]});
      return;
    }

    if (key) {
      resolve(lounger.config.sources.config.data[key]);
      return;
    }

    resolve(fs.readFileSync(lounger.config.sources));
  });
}
```

Modifying the config is done by the set function. It takes a key and a value, calls set on the config-chain object, and resolves the promise after the values are written to the disk:

```
function set (key, value) {
  return new Promise((resolve, reject) => {
    if (!key && !value) {
      reject(new Error('key and value required'));
      return;
    }

    lounger.config.set(key, value, 'config');
    lounger.config.on('save', () => {
      resolve();
    });

    lounger.config.save('config');
  });
}
```

As a last step, we have to expose both commands:

```
exports.api = {
  get: get,
  set: set
};
```

We build the CLI functionality on top of our API functions. The main difference between the API and CLI functions is that the CLI function has side effects for the get command: it prints the result to the console. We also add some nice error messages to make it easier for our users to use. They get instructions on how to run the command if they don't use it properly:

```
exports.cli = cli;
function cli (cmd, key, value) {
```

```
  return new Promise((resolve, reject) => {

    function getUsageError () {
      const err = new Error([
        'Usage:',
        '',
        'lounger config get [<key>]',
        'lounger config set <key> <value>',
      ].join('\n'));
      err.type = 'EUSAGE';
      return err;
    }

    if (!cmd || (cmd !== 'get' && cmd !== 'set')) {
      const err = getUsageError();
      return reject(err);
    }

    if (cmd === 'get') {
      return get(key).then((result) => {
        console.log(result);
      }).catch(reject);
    }

    if (cmd === 'set') {
      if (!key && !value) {
        const err = getUsageError();
        return reject(err);
      }
      return set(key, value).catch(reject);
    }
  });
}
```

Great! We have a config command now! Here is our config command in action:

```
$ lounger config set json true
$ lounger config set foo bar

$ lounger config get
{ json: true, foo: 'bar' }
$ lounger config get json
{ json: true }
```

We fulfilled all points and are ready for an initial release!

Note   The code for this section is at `sourcecode/config`.

Our First Release and Tips

You can publish open source modules after registering an account at the npm registry. After registering the account, you just have to type `npm publish` to publish your module to the registry. Before we publish lounger, I want to mention that there are some nice ways to optimize the published packages. In this section, I will explain how to optimize your package in terms of size and installation time.

One way to keep the installation size small is to add an `.npmignore` file to the root directory. It works like a `.gitignore` file, and npm won't include the listed files and directories in the published package.

Depending on the types of the files that aren't needed when using the module, we can save a lot of space on the hard disks of our users. We can save them a lot of bandwidth too.

We can save some space by excluding our unit and integration tests as well as the source for the compiled documentation:

```
/test/
/docs/
build.js

.DS_Store
npm-debug.log
```

Another great way to speed up installation time is to include all production dependencies in the published module. We can tell npm to bundle them with our module by adding them as bundleDependencies to our package.json:

```
"bundleDependencies": [
  "config-chain",
  "nopt",
  "npmlog",
  "opener",
  "osenv",
  "request"
],
```

Bundling the dependencies reduces the installation time a lot, as we omit all the small HTTP requests for each dependency and their dependencies during installation. With the current npm, installation time is reduced from 20 seconds to 5 seconds for a broadband connection. Bundling the dependencies also makes sure that our package is still installable even if a module was unpublished.

When we now run npm publish, we will publish a highly optimized version of our package.

Note   The code for this section is at `sourcecode/first-release`.

Summary

In this chapter, we made a lot of progress. We enhanced the usability of our client. We also created systems for help and configuration. The command-line client supports JSON output and shortcuts. Oh, and I have to congratulate you! You made your first release of the tool. Along the way, you've learned a few tricks to enhance the installation experience for the user. This gives you a solid foundation for the next chapter, where we'll cover streams to handle large amounts of data.

CHAPTER 4

Migrating Large Amounts of Data by Using Streams

In the preceding chapter, we made sure that our users will enjoy our CLI. We also published our first release. Now we want to take a look at a more advanced topic: streams. Streams are a very powerful feature in Node.js for processing large amounts of data. With traditional buffering, we quickly run into memory problems, because all the data just doesn't fit into the memory of the computer. Streams enable us to process data in small slices. Node.js streams work like Unix streams on the terminal, where you pipe data from a producer into a consumer by using the pipe symbol (|). We will take a look at how piping works by exploring the cat command. Afterward, we will create our own streams and integrate them into our command-line client.

© Robert Kowalski 2017
R. Kowalski, *The CLI Book*, https://doi.org/10.1007/978-1-4842-3177-7_4

The cat Command

The `cat` program prints the content of files to `stdout`. In this example, I am piping the output of the `cat` program into `tr` to change all letters from our `package.json` to uppercase letters:

```
$ cat sourcecode/first-release/package.json | tr 'a-z' 'A-Z'
```

It works with all output on `stdout`:

```
$ echo "i shout?" | tr 'a-z' 'A-Z'
```

Streams in Unix and in Node.js enable us to compose small programs or modules that do one thing well to get our task done. They handle backpressure, which means that a fast producer will automatically slow down if it is piped into a slow consumer.

The most used streams in Node are the `Readable`, `Writable`, and `Transform` streams. They are base classes that can be used to build your own custom streams. Other stream types, such as the `Duplex` stream and the `Passthrough` stream, aren't covered in the book. The `Readable` stream is used to read input data, the `Transform` stream is usually used to modify chunks of data, and the `Writable` stream accepts data to write it somewhere (for example, into a file).

Today we will write a command that will use streams for piping data from CSV files into CouchDB/PouchDB. We could also write an importer to migrate data from a database (for example, Postgres or MongoDB), but with plain CSV files, we don't have to install a new database. The principle applies to both source types, files, and databases. At the end of the chapter, I will provide a link to an example for a Node.js stream pipeline that migrates data from MongoDB to CouchDB/PouchDB.

The First Stream

Building streams can be a bit tricky sometimes. We start by creating the file `stream-example.js` in the root dir of our module.

Our first iteration will output our CSV contents to `stdout`. We will use it to learn how streams work and build our importer on top of it later. To develop, we need a CSV file; we can save it to `test/fixtures/test.csv`:

```
time;location
march;austin,us
april;boston,us
october;bristol,uk
february;hermigua,es
march;hermigua,es
april;havana,cu
```

Luckily, we don't have to write our own streaming CSV parser:

```
$ npm install --save csv-parse
```

We require the `fs` and `util` modules. The `fs` module is needed to read the CSV file from disk. We also need to require the CSV parser:

```
const parse = require('csv-parse');
const fs = require('fs');
const Transform = require('stream').Transform;
```

Our custom stream, called `MyTransformStream`, inherits from `stream.Transform`. We set the stream into `objectMode` to be able to process the JSON input from the CSV parser:

```
class MyTransformStream extends Transform {
  constructor (options = { objectMode: true }) {
```

```
  options.objectMode = true;

  super(options);
 }

}
```

A `Transform` stream has to implement one method: `_transform`. This method is part of the class we just created and called for every chunk of data that we are processing. In the `_transform` method, we can transform the chunks to something new. The transformed data is then pushed to the next consumer by using `this.push`. Once we are finished, we call the `done` callback to signal that we are finished with this chunk. Right now, we just want to take a look at what a chunk looks like:

```
_transform (chunk, encoding, done) {
  console.log('chunk: ', chunk);

  this.push(chunk);

  done();
}
```

As a last step, we have to pipe the CSV file into the CSV parser, and the parsed output into our custom stream:

```
const opts = {comment: '#', delimiter: ';', columns: true};
const parser = parse(opts);
const input = fs.createReadStream(__dirname + '/test/fixtures/
test.csv');

input
  .pipe(parser)
  .pipe(new MyTransformStream());
```

When we now run node `streams-example.js`, we get this output:

```
$ node streams-example.js
chunk:  { time: 'march', location: 'austin,us' }
chunk:  { time: 'april', location: 'boston,us' }
chunk:  { time: 'october', location: 'bristol,uk' }
chunk:  { time: 'february', location: 'hermigua,es' }
chunk:  { time: 'march', location: 'hermigua,es' }
chunk:  { time: 'april', location: 'havana,cu' }
```

Every chunk is a JSON object. Every time we call done and there is still input produced, _transform is called with the next chunk. We could take every chunk and post it against the CouchDB / HTTP API now. We would keep our memory footprint super low, but we would also send a lot of HTTP requests, and the whole migration would take a long time. A healthy compromise is to buffer a few chunks and post them against the bulk APIs of CouchDB/PouchDB. This way, we don't buffer all existing data and run out of memory. We also will be finished earlier with our import, as we don't have to send so many HTTP requests.

Note   The code for this section can be found at `sourcecode/ streams/streams-example.js`.

The Transform and Writable Stream

For our next stream, we will create the file `streams-bulk-example.js` in the root directory of lounger. It will take the objects from the CSV parsing stream and buffer them. At a given limit, it will pass the buffered objects to the next consumer. The result passed to the next consumer is ready to get posted against the CouchDB/PouchDB bulk docs API endpoint. The CouchDB/ PouchDB bulk API accepts an array of objects wrapped with `{"docs": []}`.

Creating a Wrapping Transform Stream

We start with the same set of modules to develop the Transform stream:

```
const parse = require('csv-parse');
const fs = require('fs');
const Transform = require('stream').Transform;
```

The name of our stream will be TransformToBulkDocs and it will take options as an object. Using the options, we can specify the number of documents to buffer:

```
class TransformToBulkDocs extends Transform {
  constructor (options = { objectMode: true, bufferedDocCount:
  200 }) {
    options.objectMode = true;

    super(options);
```

The empty array for `this.buffer` will be our buffer:

```
this.buffer = [];
this.bufferedDocCount = options.bufferedDocCount;
```

Here is the whole class without the _transform method:

```
class TransformToBulkDocs extends Transform {
  constructor (options = { objectMode: true, bufferedDocCount:
200 }) {
    options.objectMode = true;

    super(options);

    this.buffer = [];
    this.bufferedDocCount = options.bufferedDocCount;
  }
}
```

In the _transform method, we add every chunk to our buffer:

```
_transform (chunk, encoding, done) {
  this.buffer.push(chunk);
```

If the buffer has grown big enough, we call the method this.push, which we inherited from the base Transform stream. this.push(args) tells Node that we want to pass args to the next consumer in our stream pipeline. We then empty the buffer for new data that might arrive:

```
  if (this.buffer.length >= this.bufferedDocCount) {
    this.push({docs: this.buffer});
    this.buffer = [];
  }

  done();
}
```

Here is the whole _transform method:

```
_transform (chunk, encoding, done) {
  this.buffer.push(chunk);
  if (this.buffer.length >= this.bufferedDocCount) {
    this.push({docs: this.buffer});
    this.buffer = [];
  }

  done();
}
```

The last part of our file is almost identical to our first streams example:

```
const opts = {comment: '#', delimiter: ';', columns: true};
const parser = parse(opts);
const input = fs.createReadStream(__dirname + '/test/fixtures/
test.csv');
```

```
input
  .pipe(parser)
  .pipe(new TransformToBulkDocs());
```

We add a temporary `console.log` to our code to see if it works:

```
if (this.buffer.length >= this.bufferedDocCount) {
  this.push({docs: this.buffer});
  console.log({docs: this.buffer});
  this.buffer = [];
}
```

When we run node `streams-bulk-example.js,` we see that it doesn't work! Why?

The problem is that we don't have enough documents to reach the default document count of 200. The same applies to the remaining documents of a set. If we have 250 initial documents as input, the first 200 are pushed to the next consumer, but the remaining 50 are lost. Luckily, the Node.js developers were aware of the problem and provided the `_flush` method. Unlike the `_transform` method, the `_flush` method doesn't have to be implemented to make a `Transform` stream work. Instead, we can choose to implement it if we need it.

The `_flush` method of a `Transform` class will get called at the very end, after all data is consumed by the stream, but before the stream emits the end event that signals the end of the stream. `_flush` will get called at the very end, and if we still have a few buffered documents, we push them to the next consumer:

```
_flush (done) {
  this.buffer.length && this.push({docs: this.buffer});
  done();
}
```

That's our first custom stream! Don't forget to remove the `console.log` call we added!

The next consumer in our pipeline will take the collected documents and post them against the CouchDB/PouchDB bulk docs endpoint. As the streams are able to handle backpressure, the other streams will wait until we've successfully added the documents to CouchDB/PouchDB. They will continue to pass us data down the pipeline after we are able to pull in the next collection of documents.

The next stream we will build accepts the data from the `Transform` stream and writes it into the database. We will add that stream next.

Piping the Results into a Writable Stream

We will now pipe the data into a `Writable` stream and add it to our `streams-bulk-example.js` file. `Writable` streams can accept data from consumers and direct the data to a new location. A `Writable` file stream would write in chunks to the hard disk.

```
const Writable = require('stream').Writable;
```

Our `Writable` stream needs to know where to put the data, so we will need to pass it the database URL. As the methods of the stream are called for each chunk, we have to store the passed URL as `this.url`:

```
class CouchBulkImporter extends Writable {
  constructor (options) {
    if (!options) {
      options = {};
    }

    if (!options.url) {
      const msg = [
        'options.url must be set',
        'example:',
        "new CouchBulkImporter({url: 'http://localhost:5984/
        baseball'})"
```

```
    ].join('\n')
    throw new Error(msg);
  }

  options.objectMode = true;

  super(options);

  // sanitise url, remove trailing slash
  this.url = options.url.replace(/\/$/, '');
  }
}
```

To implement a child of a Writable stream, we have to implement the
_write method. Like the _transform method of the Transform stream, the
_write method is called for every chunk that is passed to the stream from
the previous producer. In our case, we send the JSON chunks as JSON to
the database by using request. After we send the data successfully to the
/_bulk_docs API endpoint, we call the done callback to signal that we are
ready for a new chunk:

```
_write (chunk, enc, done) {
  request({
    json: true,
    uri: this.url + '/_bulk_docs',
    method: 'POST',
    body: chunk
  }, function (err, res, body) {
    if (err) {
      return done(err);
    }

    if (!/^2../.test(res.statusCode)) {
      const msg = 'CouchDB server answered: \n Status: ' +
```

```
      res.statusCode + '\n Body: ' + JSON.stringify(body);
    return done(new Error(msg));
  }

  done();
});
}
```

We also have to require request in our file:

```
const request = require('request');
```

To use the stream, we have to pipe the data into it. We update the last section of streams-bulk-example.js:

```
input
  .pipe(parser)
  .pipe(new TransformToBulkDocs())
  .pipe(new CouchBulkImporter({url: 'http://127.0.0.1:5984/
  travel'}));
```

After we create the database travel and run our script, we import the CSV:

```
$ curl -X PUT http://localhost:5984/travel
{"ok":true}
$ node streams-bulk-example.js
$ curl http://localhost:5984/travel/_all_docs
{"total_rows":6,"offset":0,"rows":[{"id":"3444bf7c-
65c0-438f-f8e8-7f55124f1736","key":"3444bf7c-65c0-438f-
f8e8-7f55124f1736","value":{"rev":"1-37fcd2e5b409398
05b8e043da44f9b1d"}},{"id":"568c3b0f-78fe-43a2-9eac-
06620cfaa595","key":"568c3b0f-78fe-43a2-9eac-06620cfaa595",
"value":{"rev":"1-e047788bac9aada0564fc928642d3960"}},
{"id":"5d170e63-d845-4e45-f760-97e30cbc4b21","key":
```

"5d170e63-d845-4e45-f760-97e30cbc4b21","value":{"rev":
"1-6f1794e4eb24b60665fe02c2624d53eb"}},{"id":"9cd34a61-8a48-
4b88-afbf-7fd6e3c9cf42","key":"9cd34a61-8a48-4b88-afbf-
7fd6e3c9cf42","value":{"rev":"1-747b11a103cc0fe31d1c546ef70d69c
0"}},{"id":"cc7da504-438a-40c1-842b-4722b63c9a37","key":
"cc7da504-438a-40c1-842b-4722b63c9a37","value":{"rev":
"1-0f9e7add8b7fbb773dc7d3081475d855"}},{"id":
"f09811c5-43ec-4a6d-bd3b-b34b3674676d","key":
"f09811c5-43ec-4a6d-bd3b-b34b3674676d","value":
{"rev":"1-d677c5bbbee1bbbe45f6128a9cf1fe8d"}}]}

We can access a single document by using one of the IDs that the database automatically assigned to each document:

```
$ curl http://localhost:5984/travel/3444bf7c-65c0-438f-f8e8-
7f55124f1736
{"time":"february","location":"hermigua,es","_id":"3444bf7c-
65c0-438f-f8e8-7f55124f1736","_rev":"1-37fcd2e5b40939805b8e043d
a44f9b1d"}
```

Looks great! Seems we have everything in place to use our low-level streaming functions in the command-line client.

Note   The code for this section is located at `sourcecode/`
`streams/streams-bulk-example.js`.

The Streaming Import Command

For the remainder of the chapter, we will reuse the custom stream implementation that we just created. In the real world, I would create two modules for our two streams to make them reusable across multiple projects. For now, we can copy the code for the CouchBulkImporter and the TransformToBulkDocs streams into lib/csv.js, which will be the home of our import command:

```
const parse = require('csv-parse');
const fs = require('fs');
const Transform = require('stream').Transform;
const util = require('util');
const Writable = require('stream').Writable;
const request = require('request');
const lounger = require('./lounger.js');

class TransformToBulkDocs extends Transform {
  constructor (options) {
    if (!options) {
      options = {};
    }

    if (!options.bufferedDocCount) {
      options.bufferedDocCount = 200;
    }

    options.objectMode = true;

    super(options);

    this.buffer = [];
    this.bufferedDocCount = options.bufferedDocCount;
  }
```

```
  _transform (chunk, encoding, done) {
    this.buffer.push(chunk);
    if (this.buffer.length >= this.bufferedDocCount) {
      this.push({docs: this.buffer});
      this.buffer = [];
    }

    done();
  }

  _flush (done) {

    this.buffer.length && this.push({docs: this.buffer});
    done();
  }
}

class CouchBulkImporter extends Writable {
  constructor (options) {
    if (!options) {
      options = {};
    }

    if (!options.url) {
      const msg = [
        'options.url must be set',
        'example:',
        "new CouchBulkImporter({url: 'http://localhost:5984/
        baseball'})"
      ].join('\n')
      throw new Error(msg);
    }
```

```
  options.objectMode = true;

  super(options);

  // sanitize url, remove trailing slash
  this.url = options.url.replace(/\/$/, '');
}

_write (chunk, enc, done) {
  request({
    json: true,
    uri: this.url + '/_bulk_docs',
    method: 'POST',
    body: chunk
  }, function (err, res, body) {
    if (err) {
      return done(err);
    }

    if (!/^2../.test(res.statusCode)) {
      const msg = 'CouchDB server answered: \n Status: ' +
        res.statusCode + '\n Body: ' + JSON.stringify(body);
      return done(new Error(msg));
    }

    done();
  });
}
}
```

Designing the Command

Let's think a bit about the command we are going to build. A CSV can have different delimiters; some use semicolons as a delimiter, whereas others use commas or tabs. The symbols to denote a comment can also change. In our previous implementations, we used fixed values:

```
const opts = {comment: '#', delimiter: ';', columns: true};
```

For a real-world use case, the symbols for the delimiter and comment must be configurable. The CSV input is usually a file.

Here is a possible CLI:

```
$ lounger csv transfer <file> <database> [--delimiter=;]
[--comment=#] [--chunksize=200]
```

The csv command is open to extension and can host all CSV-related commands in the future. The command reads quite nicely and is easy to remember: `lounger csv transfer <file> <database>` reads almost as `lounger [do] csv transfer [from] <file> [to] <database>`. Sane defaults help us avoid passing optional modifiers at all, but in case we need to modify them, we can change every important aspect of our import.

I'm not sure whether you noticed it, but when we played with our streams, we would have had to create the target database by using curl in advance. It would be handy if our CLI users didn't have to create the target database on their own. Our goal is to help them solve their tasks as quickly and easily as possible, so we should automatically create databases as necessary. As a next step, we will add a helper to create the database.

Creating the Target Database

To make the life of our users easier, we will add a function that creates the target database. This way, we can ensure that the command workflow has no major obstacles. The `createTargetDatabase` function is a helper

function that wraps request into a promise. If the database is created
(HTTP code 201 or 200) or the database exists already (HTTP code 412),
we resolve; all other states lead to rejection of the promise:

```
function createTargetDatabase (url) {
  return new Promise((resolve, reject) => {
    request({
      json: true,
      uri: url,
      method: 'PUT',
      body: {}
    }, function (er, res, body) {
      if (er && (er.code === 'ECONNREFUSED' || er.code ===
      'ENOTFOUND')) {
        const err = new Error(
          'Could not connect to ' + url + '. Please check if
          the database is offline'
        );
        err.type = 'EUSAGE';
        return reject(err);
      }

      if (er) {
        return reject(er);
      }

      const code = res.statusCode;

      if (code !== 200 && code !== 201 && code !== 412) {
        const msg = 'CouchDB server answered: \n Status: ' +
          res.statusCode + '\n Body: ' + JSON.stringify(body);
        return reject(new Error(msg));
      }
```

```
    resolve();
  });
 });
}
```

In case of an ECONNREFUSED or ENOTFOUND error, we can safely assume that the database is currently offline and ask the user to see whether the database is available. I can't stress enough how important proper error handling is. Take this example, where we are getting back ECONNREFUSED:

```
$ ./bin/lounger-cli csv transfer test/fixtures/test.csv
http://127.0.0.1:1337/testimport
ERR! connect ECONNREFUSED 127.0.0.1:5984
ERR! Error: connect ECONNREFUSED 127.0.0.1:5984
ERR!     at Object.exports._errnoException (util.js:870:11)
ERR!     at exports._exceptionWithHostPort (util.js:893:20)
ERR!     at TCPConnectWrap.afterConnect [as oncomplete]
(net.js:1063:14)
ERR!
ERR!
ERR! lounger: 1.0.0 node: v9.1.0
ERR! please open an issue including this log on http://example.
com/lounger/issues
```

Depending on how much our users have used Node.js before, they might be very puzzled. The only way for them to continue would be to ask a search engine or to open an issue. After receiving the issue, our boring job would be to close the issue and tell them that they probably had a typo in their URL.

After writing the createTargetDatabase function, we should have all our supporting functions in place. As usual, we start to implement the main CLI functions by implementing the API command, which we will then wrap with our CLI function.

The delimiter and comment options are defined in the config file or are passed on the command line. To know what their values are, we have to interact with lounger.config. To access lounger.config, we have to require it:

```
const lounger = require('./lounger.js');
```

The main API function checks whether all necessary arguments were provided and applies defaults if no configuration was passed in from the config file or on the command line. We create the database in case it does not exist yet and delegate to the importFromCsvFile helper function:

```
exports.api = {
  transfer: bulkdocsImport
};

function bulkdocsImport (file, targetDb) {
  return new Promise((resolve, reject) => {
    const opts = {};

    if (!file && !targetDb) {
      return reject(new Error('file and/or targetDb argument
      missing'));
    }

    opts.delimiter = lounger.config.get('delimiter') || ';';
    opts.comment = lounger.config.get('comment') || '#';
    opts.chunksize = lounger.config.get('chunksize') || 200;

    createTargetDatabase(targetDb)
      .then(() => {
        return importFromCsvFile(file, targetDb, opts);
      }).catch(reject);
  });
}
```

importFromCsvFile accepts the source CSV file, URL, and options, and creates the stream pipeline. The main difference from our previous code in streams-example.js is that we have proper error handling in place to catch all errors:

```
function importFromCsvFile (file, url, opts) {
  return new Promise((resolve, reject) => {
    const options = {comment: opts.comment, delimiter: opts.
    delimiter, columns: true};
    const parser = parse(options);
    const input = fs.createReadStream(file);

    input
      .pipe(parser)
      .on('error', reject)
      .pipe(new TransformToBulkDocs({bufferedDocCount: opts.
      chunksize}))
      .on('error', reject)
      .pipe(new CouchBulkImporter({url: url}))
      .on('error', reject);
  });
}
```

The CLI function finally wraps our API method and adds friendly error messages:

```
exports.cli = importCli;
function importCli (cmd, file, target) {
  return new Promise((resolve, reject) => {
    if (!cmd || cmd !== 'transfer' || !file || !target) {
      const err = new Error(
        'Usage: lounger csv transfer <file> <database>
        [--delimiter=;] [--comment=#] [--chunksize=200]'
      );
```

```
    err.type = 'EUSAGE';
    return reject(err);
  }

  return bulkdocsImport(file, target).catch(reject);
});
}
```

We introduced three new options: delimiter, comment, and chunksize. lounger.config enables our users to set default values by using the config file. In addition, we have to take care that the options are parsed on the command line. In bin/lounger-cli, we have to register our optional arguments to nopt:

```
const parsed = nopt({
  'json': [Boolean],
  'delimiter': [String],
  'comment': [String],
  'chunksize': [Number]
}, {'j': '--json'}, process.argv, 2);
```

That's it! We created a command that is able to stream large amounts of data into our database.

If you are interested in a stream pipeline that would stream data from MongoDB to CouchDB, you can take a look at https://github.com/robertkowalski/couchbulkimporter/blob/master/examples/mongo.js.

Note   The code for this section is at sourcecode/streams. Enjoy!

Summary

With streams, we have a way to work with large amounts of data that don't fit into memory. Based on streams, we built a data importer that can handle very large amounts of data. As a last step, we integrated everything into the command-line client. Hopefully, you enjoyed our adventure into streams!

APPENDIX A

Tips and Tricks

This short appendix provides some tips and tricks regarding Node.js development in general.

Testing

With proper unit and integration tests in place, ensure that new features or bug fixes don't introduce regressions. A lot of great services provide a hosted continuous integration (CI) environment. They can test every pull request before it is merged, which makes reviewing code a lot easier. A popular service for hosted CI is Travis CI. Travis CI is free for open source projects.

Semantic Versioning with SemVer

I recommend following semantic versioning with SemVer (`http://semver.org/`). SemVer divides the version number of a release into three areas: MAJOR.MINOR.PATCH. The version 3.5.8 would have 3 as the MAJOR version level, 5 as the MINOR version level, and 8 as the PATCH level. If a new release includes a breaking change, the MAJOR version number is bumped. A new feature would need just a minor version bump, and bug fixes would require a bump of only the PATCH section.

© Robert Kowalski 2017
R. Kowalski, *The CLI Book*, https://doi.org/10.1007/978-1-4842-3177-7

Here's an example: My package has version 3.5.7. I add a new feature that does not break backward compatibility. My next release would be 3.6.0.

This way, your users have an idea of whether a release might break their production code (MAJOR), contains a new feature (MINOR), or include a bug fix (PATCH). A great tool to help you make the right decision for the next version bump is semantic-release (`www.npmjs.com/package/semantic-release`).

Greenkeeper

Keeping track of which dependencies of your project have a new version and need to be updated can be tedious. The update itself (bumping the version number in the `package.json file`) is not the most interesting task on earth, either. A new and exciting service is `http://greenkeeper.io`. Once you register it for your project, it will send you pull requests with updated versions of your dependencies. If you have a test suite in place and everything is "green," you just have to merge the pull request from the Greenkeeper bot.

Testing and a CI service that automatically runs the tests, SemVer, and Greenkeeper really show their strengths when combined.

Index

A, B

API in command-line client, 10, 11

C

Command-line interface (CLI)
   CLI client, 3
   command-line tool, 2
   configuration
      config-chain, 73
      config object, 74
      creation, 71–72
      editing, 76–78, 80
      ini-formatted files, 72
   documentation
      (*see* Documentation, CLI)
   error handling, 7–8
      bugs property, 45
      command-line
         client, 40, 45
      isonline command, 39
      lib/isonline.js., 40
      nonexistent function, 44
      package.json, 45
      stacktraces, 39
      usage errors, 41–42, 44
      validations, 46

Git project, 5
helper functions, 69–70
JSON support and
      shorthand, 47, 49
list of commands, 66–67
$ lounger, 66
man page, 4
npm publish, 6
opener module, 68
principles, 2
spawn command, 69
Continuous integration (CI), 105

D

Database administration tool
   booting, 31–37
   command-line client, 29–30
   command-line tool, 15
   CouchDB and PouchDB, 22
   database server, 21
      curl, 18
      file-watcher error, 19–20
      PouchDB database
         server, 17–18
      setting up, 16
      troubleshooting, 18
   ecosystem, 23, 25–26

© Robert Kowalski 2017
R. Kowalski, *The CLI Book*, https://doi.org/10.1007/978-1-4842-3177-7

Database administration tool (*cont.*)
   isonline Command, 26–27, 29
   isonline.js file, 29
   Node.js, 16
   package.json file, 22
Documentation, CLI
   buildMan(), 56
   build script, 60, 62–63, 65
   detailed description, 50
   doc/cli/lounger-isonline.md, 51
   folder structure, 52
   fs module, 54
   fs.writeFileSync, 55
   getSources function, 53
   HTML Output, 58, 60
   JavaScript, 52
   lounger.commands, 50
   man pages, 56
   man-pages directory, 56–57
   Markdown files, 53
   Node.js platform, 52, 53
   npm script, 56
   optional command, 51
   scripts section, 56
   sources object, 53
Duplex stream, 84

E, F

Error handling, 7–8
   bugs property, 45
   command-line client, 40, 45
   isonline command, 39
   lib/isonline.js., 40

nonexistent function, 44
package.json, 45
stacktraces, 39
usage errors, 41–42, 44
validations, 46

G, H, I, J, K, L

Greenkeeper, 106

M, N, O

MyTransformStream, 85

P, Q, R

Passthrough stream, 84
Power users
   command-line client, 10, 12
   configuration, 11–12
   exit codes, 9
   JSON Output, 10
   scripting, 9
   shortcuts, 9

S

Semantic versioning, 105
Streams
   cat command, 84
   console.log, 90
   CouchDB/PouchDB, 91
   custom stream, 86
   _flush method, 90

fs and util modules, 85
import command
    CouchBulkImporter, 95–97
    creation, database, 98,
      100–103
    designing, 98
    TransformToBulk
      Docs, 95–97
MyTransformStream, 85
node streams-bulk-example.js, 90
node streams-example.js, 87

test/fixtures/test.csv, 85
transform method, 88–89
transform stream, 88
TransformToBulkDocs, 88
Writable stream, 91, 93–94

T, U, V, W, X, Y, Z

Test-driven
      development (TDD), 25
Transform stream, 84

Get the eBook for only $5!

Why limit yourself?

With most of our titles available in both PDF and ePUB format, you can access your content wherever and however you wish—on your PC, phone, tablet, or reader.

Since you've purchased this print book, we are happy to offer you the eBook for just $5.

To learn more, go to http://www.apress.com/companion or contact support@apress.com.

Apress®

Printed in the United States
By Bookmasters